My

My Shadow

Fewer Triggers,
Better Parenting, Less Guilt

Anthony Martino

My Kid, My Shadow

Fewer Triggers, Better Parenting, Less Guilt

Published in the United States of America by Vangelo Media; www.vangelomedia.com. Send inquiries to info@vangelomedia.com.

Publisher's Cataloging-in-Publication data

Martino, Anthony.

  My Kid, My Shadow : Fewer Triggers, Better Parenting, Less Guilt / Anthony Martino.

  ISBN: 978-1-940604-32-9

Summary: My Kid, My Shadow, describes a 7 step process to uncover the root cause of parental triggers and resolve them through shadow integration. The book delves deeply into the unconscious mechanisms that ignite parental triggers, influence parenting decisions, and prohibit parents from changing how they parent. Ultimately, this is a book of self-awareness and self-discovery. It is based on Carl Jung's work on shadow identification and shadow integration, and it describes these concepts in simple, pragmatic ways.

*To my beautiful wife
who has always stood by my side
with a helping hand and open heart.*

Chapters

Opening.....3

My Kid, My Fault?.....9

What We Want For Our Children.....15

Seven Steps.....19

Our Children And Our Triggers.....25

Step 1: It's All About You.....32

Step 2: A Journey Through Shadows.....40

Shadows Are Not Good Or Bad.....47

Step 3: An Unknown Life.....53

Step 4: Mirror, Mirror.....59

Step 5: Why Do They Trigger Me?.....66

Mindfulness.....79

Step 5: See Your Shadow.....88

Blame, Shame, And Guilt.....104

Sorting Things Out.....115

Step 6: Integration And Wholeness.....122

Step 7: Share The Knowledge.....139

Your Hero's Journey Of Self-discovery.....147

Opening

"We must be willing to let go of the life we planned so as to have the life that is waiting for us."

Joseph Campbell

"I abandoned her."

The pain of guilt pierced my heart as I sat there, stunned and weeping. My mind kept spinning as I mumbled to myself ...

"I was not there when my beautiful baby girl needed me most. I abandoned her and didn't even know she needed me. I abandoned her. I abandoned her. I did not know. I did not know my daughter was alone."

The pain was almost unbearable; the wound was deep. The realization that I did this to my Genevieve covered me in guilt and shame.

"My baby suffers this pain because of me. I did this to her, just like my mother did it to me. How could I have been so blind? How? What is wrong with me? Why didn't she ask me for help?"

A second thrust of guilt pierced my heart as I realized that she didn't ask for help because she is just like me.

I sat there talking to myself, "She did what I would do, suffer in silence. I never ask anyone for help. She learned this from me. She knows that I don't respect needy people. She didn't want me there when she needed me most because she would rather be alone than have me lose respect for her."

It became clear to me that I had unwittingly passed these unhealthy behaviors to my daughter. The same ones my mother passed on to me. I became furious as I contemplated

3

this reality. I was not mad at my mother, nor myself, and certainly not angry at my beautiful baby girl. I was upset at the insidious nature of this reality. It is like a virus is sitting in my unconscious mind waiting for the perfect opportunity to infect my twins.

My anger quickly converted to determination. I was going to stop this once and for all. This burden will stop with Genevieve, and it will not be passed down to my grandchildren if I am lucky enough to have any.

A vivid memory of my wife's pregnancy popped into my head. I recalled the awe I felt the first time I placed my hand on her tummy and could feel my babies wiggling in their mother's womb. I remembered the promises I made to them that day, many promises about their future. But the most significant promise I made was that I would protect them at all costs. They would never need to worry. There is nothing that I cannot endure for them. They will be safe and protected as long as I am alive.

But I failed. I failed my Genevieve. I inadvertently hurt her by simply being me, the dad who was incapable of seeing her need. That was the moment when I realized that I must act now and figure this whole crazy thing out. I had to find out why I was not the dad she needed. I had to find a remedy for my unhealthy behaviors, so my children don't repeat the same mistakes. This book documents the things I learned in pursuit of that remedy. A remedy I want to share with you and your family.

Before we begin, I'd like to take a short pause to cover two topics. The first topic is to visualize the future, and the second is to describe the context in which this book is written. First, I'd like you to imagine that you are living in a future where you come to know who you are and why. A future where you no longer doubt yourself, and you know that you are worthy. A future where you forgive yourself, your parents, and your children. A future where you are courageous, vulnerable, and strong. A future where the relationships you have with your family members are real, meaningful, safe, and loving. A future where you love yourself unconditionally. I ask that you imagine this future because it can be yours if you dare to pursue it.

The second topic is the background information you will need to understand the context in which this book has been written. The odd thing about this information is that it contains a few 'nots.' By that, I mean, I must describe what things are not as opposed to what they are. For instance, I'd like to introduce myself, but I can't. I have written this book under the pen name Anthony Martino. I did this to protect my family's anonymity. That is because this book is an extension of a memoir I wrote a few years back that detailed some very personal information that my family wants to keep private.

I wrote that book under the same pseudonym to honor their request and preserve my family's privacy. I wish there were another way to protect my family and also be true to you, but I know of no other options. As background for who I am, let me simply say that I am a relatively typical guy in my early sixties. I'm industrious and compassionate. I live with my wife and children in a suburb of an east coast city in North America. Most people enjoy my company, and I enjoy them as well. I am not much different than you. Maybe older, maybe younger, but very much the same.

This book was conceived from a spark of light that illuminated my soul during a two-week consciousness retreat I attended a year or so ago. As described in the first few pages, that spark was ignited when I realized that I had played an essential role in screwing up my kids.

This was the third consciousness retreat that I had attended over a nine-year period of time. I have and continue to do deep consciousness work as part of my journey of self-discovery and individuation. This spark of enlightenment occurred near the end of the retreat when I figured out that the negative impact I had on my children is not only a normal part of parenting; it is also fixable. Not only is it repairable, but my consciousness work already incorporates the methods needed to help me guide my children. I realized I could teach these skills to my children in a way that they would accept. When I returned home from the retreat, I had compelling, in-depth, and rewarding discussions with my children. The idea of writing this book did not occur to me for another eight months.

Earlier I mentioned that there were a few 'nots' I need to mention to you. Here is another one; you don't have to be a parent to benefit from this book. This book is just as relevant to non-parents as it is to parents because it is ultimately about self-discovery and self-awareness. I believe anyone searching for self-awareness will find the messages and techniques described in this book of life-long value.

For those of you who do not have children, I suggest you read this book from the perspective of a child who is reading about the life they have had with their parents. For those of you with children, please read the book from the perspective of being a parent.

One of my goals in writing this book is to help you find peace and discover the person living beneath your public facade. I believe, through the discovery of oneself, you will develop more meaningful relationships with all of the cherished people in your life, especially with your children.

When you read the book, please keep in mind that some of the topics we will discuss will not be easy to confront. If you begin to feel upset or triggered, I ask that you honor yourself and acknowledge your feelings. I literally want you to stop reading for a moment, recognize what is going on with you, and feel what you are feeling at that moment. I would also like you to write down what you are thinking and feeling if you can. Try to do this without judgment or analysis. Simply write down the facts; nothing more, nothing less. If, for instance, you are feeling guilt, write down that you are feeling guilty about X, Y or Z. Don't try to understand, explain, or filter it.

There are two reasons for my request. The first and most important is that we too often ignore our feelings and just move on. I don't want you to do that. Take the time to honor and validate your feelings and, therefore yourself. The second is that the information you gather will be of immense value in later chapters of the book.

Honoring yourself in this way is an invaluable form of self-care, and it is an essential form of self-witnessing. Please stop and take the time to acknowledge your feelings, reaffirm your importance, declare your worthiness, and validate your existence. Remember, you are, and will forever be, one of God's beautiful creations. As such, you are worthy of recognition, acknowledgment, self-care, and love.

Journaling will be a valuable part of this book as well. So much so I have added an extra blank page at the end of each chapter for that specific purpose. Please use these blank pages to write notes, doodle, or draw. If you have a journal, feel free to use it instead. Don't hesitate to write or draw anything. Even things that seem to be disconnected from the words you are reading at the time. If an image or word pops into your mind, jot it down. I know with certainty that the words, pictures, symbols, and scribbles that seem irrelevant and disconnected will end up being quite revealing when you come back to read them later. In this regard, I have published a workbook for those of you interested in more guidance as you work your way through this book.

Finally, you need to know that I am not a medical professional. As a layman, I am not qualified to give medical or psychological advice of any kind. I intend to recount my personal experiences to you and only offer information of a general nature to help you in your quest for personal growth and self-discovery. I am in no way providing anything in the form of therapy or expert advice. If you choose to adopt any suggestion implied or stated directly, neither the publisher nor I can assume any responsibility for your actions. Please, seek the services of a qualified medical or psychological professional before undertaking any suggestions herein.

My Kid, My Fault?

"In each of us there is another whom we do not know."

Carl Jung

The title of this chapter asks if you are at fault. The answer is yes, you are at fault, but there is nothing you could have done about it. So, don't feel bad.

You messed up your kid, but they are the better for it. So, there is hope.

Your kid triggers you, and you trigger your kid. So, let's find out what is going on and why.

Parent/child triggers are the outward expression of the turmoil that exists between you and your child. Most parenting books will validate the phenomenon and offer an immediate fix for coping with it on a problem by problem and day to day basis. This book does not do that. Instead, this book goes straight to the root cause and describes how and why triggers impact you and your child. It aims to offer methods and techniques to address and resolve triggers at their core rather than focus on individual problems and issues.

As you read this book, you will come to understand how parents and children interact with each other and the reasons why children push their parent's buttons so easily. You will realize that this whole process is so very normal, and you are not the only parent struggling with it. We all are.

The good news is that there is a way to disempower the buttons your child pushes while, at the same time, strengthening the relationship you have with your child. When you learn to do this, you will become much more self-aware and more connected with yourself and your child. This book will discuss these topics along with a process for resolving the conflicts, healing the pain, and becoming whole.

But first, there must come a time of self-reflection when parents accept that their child is struggling with life because of the role they have played. Their child is unhappy, anxious, lost, troubled, or maladjusted, and they ask themselves if they are the cause. "Am I the one who has messed up my kid?"

This is a reasonable question to ask, even though most parents already know the answer. It is a question that I, too, have asked and answered. But it wasn't until I consciously accepted the harsh reality of the answer that I could feel its impact. I was distraught, as you could see on the opening page of this book. I became overwhelmed with guilt and self-doubt. 'Shoulda, woulda, coulda' thinking permeated my mind. I imagined all sorts of reasons why. Feelings of shame and blame triggered more and more guilt. A perpetual cycle of shame, blame, and guilt ensued as I felt lost and powerless to effect change. Luckily, this happened when I was at a 2-week consciousness retreat, and I had the time to process it all. This book is the result.

When most parents answer this question, they do the same kind of 'shoulda, woulda, coulda' thinking I did. They wish they had been a better parent. But I now know that is not possible. They could not have parented their child any differently than they have. Indeed, there are specific situations where a different decision would have been better, but I am not talking about problems and issues at that level. Instead, I am focusing on the root cause of the problems so we can target resolution at the source. Until parents are able to uncover the root of the problem, there is nothing they could have done to have caused a different outcome for their child. This book aims to explain how and why that is true and offers a way to resolve issues at their source.

Another thing I learned was that accepting your child with all of his flaws has everything to do with you and very little to do with your child. We will see that it is ultimately about you accepting your failings, fears, and foibles. This is because many of the issues parents have with their children are, in fact, sourced from the parent's unhappiness with themselves. Accepting those issues in yourself is the only way to accept those deficiencies in your child. This means you must learn to love yourself unconditionally and believe that you are worthy of such love.

Unconditional self-love is the necessary prerequisite to having deep, meaningful relationships with everyone in your life, especially those that are dear to you. This idea that meaningful relationships are based on loving yourself unconditionally is a foundational truth that forms one of this book's fundamental tenets. And it is one of the many topics that we will discuss, along with a process for resolving conflicts, healing the pain, and becoming whole.

For the purposes of this book, unconditional self-love is about accepting, honoring, and loving all aspects of yourself, the good, the bad, and the ugly, without limitation or constraint. To do this, you must know who you are by making your identity consciously known to you. You must know the values, morals, and beliefs that define you. And at the same time, you must be fully aware of those aspects of yourself that are inconsistent with your values, morals, and beliefs. Once you have this level of conscious self-awareness and can articulate your definition of self, including the good and the bad, you must then accept your complete identity without condition or constraint. Only then can you see your soul and love yourself with all of your beauty, splendor, failings, and flaws.

Knowing who you are and being able to articulate it is an essential skill of self-discovery. Throughout the book, we will discuss how we define ourselves so that we can identify the hidden characteristics and traits that are incompatible or incongruent with our identity. In so doing, we will find that these inconsistencies are the things that contribute to our child's struggles.

Presuming there is no underlying mental illness in your household, your child acts the way they act and believes what they believe because of the things he has learned from you. There is nothing more to it. It is a simple fact of nature that children learn from their parent's behaviors, especially those driven by their parents' unconscious mind. The things your child learns from your unconscious actions are entirely out of your control. That means there was no conscious intent on your part. You did not overtly teach your child to adopt your failings, fears, and foibles. It just happened as a natural consequence of being their parent. Those unconscious thoughts, beliefs, traits, and behaviors are the primary subject of this book.

We all know that our children are a partial reflection of us, but we usually don't understand what that actually means, nor do we fully appreciate the implications. We often idealize this reflection and imagine only the 'good stuff' about ourselves being projected upon our children. In some cases, we even project an exaggerated view of our most laudable traits onto them. We rarely, if ever, see the parts of ourselves that we are ashamed of in our children. We absolutely don't ever want those personality traits, fears, prejudices, or desires to be visible to our children, let alone projected back to us through them; yet, they are.

As you read this book, you will learn this hard truth; some of your most upsetting, hidden, and repressed behaviors, traits, and beliefs have been sown into your child's psyche. This book will help you identify those traits so that you can see the process that has taken place and understand the impact it has had on you and your child. With that knowledge, you will then be able to pursue remedies for you both. Remedies that will foster unconditional self-love, strengthen your relationship, and help make you both whole. Those remedies will be discussed in later chapters and will require self-reflection, honesty, vulnerability, empathy, compassion, and courage.

Reading this book starts you on a journey of self-discovery. A journey that will, at times, be uncomfortable. But, it will be a worthwhile undertaking because you will come to love all aspects of yourself and your child in the process. The relationship you have with your child will become fuller, richer, and more intimate. The love you have for yourself will become tangible and a source of strength and clarity of vision.

What We Want For Our Children

"The greatest tragedy of the family is the un-lived lives of the parents."

Carl Jung

Do you know a parent who has pushed their child to be the valedictorian or a daughter to be a beauty pageant queen, or maybe a son to be a football star? That parent may be trying to re-live their lost childhood hopes and dreams through their child. These three examples provide the basis for a family tragedy, as stated in the Jung quote above.

The parent who lives vicariously through their child is usually oblivious to their child's actual wants and needs. That parent's desires form a veil that blinds them from their child's reality, replacing it instead with the parent's un-lived past. So much so that the parent believes the contrary. They think they're providing exactly what the child wants by guiding them to the happiness and contentment they missed out on during their childhood.

We all have hopes and dreams for our children, and that is a good thing as long as they are consistent with the wants and needs of the child. Hopes and dreams are universally envisioned by every parent regardless of race, religion, country of origin, culture, or socioeconomic status. Our wishes for our children begin before birth and carry on almost every day of our lives. The first time we set eyes on our newborn, we see unparalleled beauty; the baby is clearly a gift from God.

In our mind's eye, this newborn holds all the potential there can possibly be for themselves and us. We promise to accompany the baby throughout his life, acting as a catalyst and protector; mentor and caregiver; parent and friend. His dreams are our dreams, and our dreams are his dreams. Deep within our hearts, we are one.

We want for our children a better, happier, healthier life with more joy, opportunities, and more significant achievements. We will do our best to make everything a possibility. We also want for our children what we did not have. And we commit to shielding them from the misfortunes, difficulties, and heartaches we endured.

We promise to protect, comfort and nourish our children no matter what. We will overcome any obstacles blocking them, or us for that matter, as we provide a safe haven for our children to grow and prosper. Nothing will stop them on their journey through life.

Many of these plans and solemn promises are in response to our childhood. We remember the circumstances and family dynamics that were unhealthy, difficult, painful, or damaging. We reject those possibilities and commit to changing the harmful family norms that were, and are, part of our lives. We vow never to repeat those same negative patterns with our children as we prepare to build an emotionally safe home for them. We promise ourselves and are confident that we will not make the same mistakes our parents made. Our fears and limitations will not befall our children because we believe we are aware of them, and we will make sure those limitations will not impact our children. In this way, we know that our children will not be hindered as we were. They will not have to endure the unhealthy, destructive family beliefs and behaviors that have been repeated over many generations.

We will do our best to shelter and redirect our children away from the unhealthy, difficult, painful, and damaging ways of our past. But the reality is we will be lucky to fulfill half of our plans and solemn promises because we can only do this for those patterns of behavior and those thoughts that we are consciously aware of. We cannot protect our children from the habits and beliefs that are held captive within our unconscious mind because we are blind to their existence and can't directly access them. Yet, those hidden thoughts and behaviors are very much alive in us. They have already had a significant impact on our lives, and they will play an essential role in our children's lives as well. Much more so than we realize. Pushing your child to be a beauty pageant queen is but one manifestation of this reality.

In short, we are unable to protect our children from the hidden, repressed traits and beliefs that lurk within our unconscious. This book's purpose is to bring those unproductive, repressed traits and beliefs forward into your consciousness so that you can ensure they do not negatively impact your child any longer.

Seven Steps

"I once was lost, but now am found,
Was blind, but now I see."

John Newton, Amazing Grace

The lyrics above from the classic American hymn 'Amazing Grace' succinctly describes the concept of self-discovery. Specifically, it is about overcoming your internal blindness so that you understand and know what has been missing from your life. It also summarizes a theme of this book; to 'find yourself', including those parts of you that are hidden and repressed. Those parts of you that have kept you from finding the real you.

The ultimate goal of this book is to help you and your child have a deep, meaningful relationship based on unconditional love and acceptance. In this way, the behaviors and beliefs that cause the discontent between you and your child will lose their negative power and impact.

This book details a seven-step process to do just that. The first five steps of the process will help you identify the core issues that are at the heart of the conflict between you and your child. The sixth step of the process focuses on helping you heal and become whole. The seventh and last step is about helping your child by describing how your child can walk through this very same process for himself.

Please do not tell your child that you are reading a book that will help him with his problems. He will immediately reject anything you say from that point forward.

Each of the seven steps is covered in one or more chapters. The first step is the most important because it requires you to acknowledge that it all begins with you. Change must start with you, first and foremost.

The second step is to recognize that there are parts of you that are entirely unknown to you. Your unconscious mind has hidden many of your traits and beliefs from you. Those traits and beliefs are so thoroughly repressed that you do not even know that they are very much alive in you.

The third step is to accept that those hidden and repressed traits and beliefs have a profound impact on your daily life. So much so that they have molded your identity in ways that are currently invisible to you. I use the term 'shadow' to refer to these hidden and repressed traits and beliefs.

The fourth step is to see your shadows reflected back to you through those you love, specifically your children but also your parents and spouse. Our loved ones often possess some of the very same shadows that we have, and they, in turn, reflect them back to us.

The fifth step is to find your shadows by recognizing that the shadows reflected back to you are yours. This step requires you to make the shadow visible and an accepted part of your definition of self, i.e., your identity.

The sixth step is the healing step. This is where I will describe how to integrate your shadows into your consciousness as a means for healing yourself and becoming whole.

The seventh and final step is to help your child follow this very same process so they too can integrate their shadows, and their relationship with you can flourish.

These seven steps will challenge you, and they will require perseverance, courage, strength, honesty, compassion, empathy, and vulnerability. To help you with this, I am sharing my personal Love and Life Meditation with the hope it calms your soul. Please read it first, then try it for yourself.

Love and Life Meditation

Before we begin the meditation, I'd like you to hold both of your hands against your chest. One hand on top of the other, as if you are holding your heart.

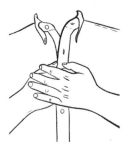

Physically holding your heart in this way is an essential part of this meditation. Notice that your hands are placed in the center of your chest, where your heart chakra is located. It is the exact same location as depicted in images of the Sacred Heart of Jesus.

Please keep in mind that love is an infinitely abundant energy that our hearts can create, give, and receive. The energy of love and life permeates the universe and is available for everyone to tap into at any time.

Now I would like you to imagine the universe imbued with the energy of unconditional love and the energy of life itself. See the energy flowing all around the cosmos connecting everything with love and life. Feel the energy of love and life surrounding the Earth and touching you, connecting you with everything, including animals and plants. When you have that image clearly in mind, I want you to remember that you are, and will forever be, one of God's beautiful creations.

Begin the meditation by closing your eyes as you breathe in and out.

With each inward breath, think the word love.

With each outward breath, think the word life.

Feel unconditional love coming into your heart with each inward breath.

Breathe the energy of life out to the universe with each outward breath.

Repeat these slow, inward, and outward breaths of love and life.

Please give this meditation a try. Do it for at least 3 minutes with or without background music. If you wish, switch the words so that you breathe in life energy, and you give loving energy with each outward breath. Or focus on only one of the energies, breathing it in and out.

Although I have laid out a seven-step process, I don't want you to think I have written the definitive 'Shadow Work For Dummies' book; I am not that smart. This is messy work, and everyone's journey is unique to them. But I want you to know that you can do this work, I have seen many people succeed, but it will take time. I am still on my journey and don't ever expect it to end. Life is too beautiful and wondrous.

These seven steps will require perseverance, courage, strength, honesty, compassion, empathy, and vulnerability. Please do not hesitate to meditate at any time when you are reading this book. I find that the Love and Life Meditation helps me calm my soul.

When I think of these seven steps, I imagine them as the graceful expression of a dance between me and those I love. It is a multi-dimensional shadow dance with the beautiful music of unconditional love guiding our movements. The first dance is between me and my inner-self. The second dance is between my loved ones and me. I hope you like to dance because I want to teach this dance to you.

I also want you to remember the ideal future you envisioned at the beginning of this book. A future where you come to know who you are and why. A future where you no longer doubt yourself, and you know that you are worthy. A future where you forgive yourself, your parents, and your children. A future where you are courageous, vulnerable, and strong. A future where your relationships with your family members are real, meaningful, safe, and loving. A future where you love yourself unconditionally.

Finally, I must caution those of you who have PTSD or a similar condition that we will discuss methods for exploring triggers later in the book. This may not be appropriate for you. Please seek the counsel of a medical professional before continuing to read any further.

Our Children And Our Triggers

"Children are educated by what the grown-up is, and not by his talk."

Carl Jung

Before we begin the seven-step process, I'd like to discuss triggers and their relationship to our children. Triggers are the touchstone we will use to understand what is going on between parents and children; and between our conscious and unconscious minds. Our objective is to understand why we are triggered and what happens with our children when we are.

In that moment of despair, when your child has again done something that has embarrassed you in public or driven you beyond the realm of crazy, you may ask yourself, "Did I make him that way? Is it my fault?" The stark reality for all parents and children without significant mental illness is yes; it is your fault. You did indeed make him that way. You, the parent, are the reason why your child does many of those unacceptable, irreverent, self-defeating, stupid, embarrassing, harmful, frightening, illegal, degrading ... activities. The surprising thing is that your child does many of them in direct response to the things they have learned from you.

I know these words are difficult to accept, and you may even reject them as you think to yourself, "There is no way it was me! I cannot be blamed for this. I would have never taught my child any of those things".

As a typical parent, you inadvertently modeled behaviors and beliefs that your child has seen and learned from every day of his life. Your child knows you inside and out. He has learned all sorts of things from you, and you have played a fundamental role in molding your child into the person he has become.

Your child has watched everything you have done and not done since birth. Children are such keen observers that they have even seen those aspects of your personality that you are oblivious to; those hidden, disowned, and repressed traits and beliefs you no longer see as a part of you. You have rejected those traits, behaviors, and beliefs and do not want anyone to know about them, especially your child. Those repressed traits are also the things that trigger you. They become the basis for the buttons your child pushes to cause a reaction in you. And your child will use those buttons to manipulate you at will. This interplay of triggers and buttons between parent and child is typical of a normal, healthy parent/child relationship.

Your child will, at times, exhibit behaviors that anger you. They will also have beliefs that you overtly reject, deny, and disapprove of. You see those traits and beliefs as quite alien and wonder where they came from and why your child has adopted them. Yet, at the same time, you will see other traits and behaviors within your child and are in awe. You see your child's innocence, beauty, intellect, and potential. You see aspects of yourself within them, especially those traits you are most proud of. You find yourself bragging to your friends about your child's accomplishments, interests, and dreams. You love your child dearly and don't understand how they have come to exhibit such extreme behaviors, both 'good' and 'bad.'

How can this dichotomy be true? How can your child be both beauty and beast? How can you beam with pride over your child and also be fed up with some of the things they say, do, or believe?

If you stop for a moment and honestly think about yourself, you will recognize that this dichotomy is alive in you as well. You wear the mask of the good parent and accomplished citizen while simultaneously possessing traits and beliefs that you hide from others, including yourself. How can you live this secret life of contradiction? How can you be both beauty and beast? These are questions that probe deeply into the human psyche.

This capacity to be both 'this and that' is an extraordinary characteristic of what it is to be a normal, healthy human being.

Understanding the 'this, and that' reality and accepting its truth is one of the prerequisites needed to comprehend your unconscious mind's complexities. We will be exploring the part of your unconscious mind that has influenced many, if not all, of your life's decisions. The same part that has molded you into the person you have become. The person, your child, has observed every day of his life and can manipulate with ease. The person from whom your child has learned many different things, including religious and political dogma, prejudices, and desires.

Your child learns from you through explicit, overt teaching as well as through subtle, unconscious communications. The subtle, unconscious messages we send are invisible to us but not to our children. The energy we radiate is a surprisingly powerful communication medium that allows your child to read even small changes in your state of mind. Subtle facial expressions or body movements also tell your child much about your mood and how you feel. These subtle observations are the things your child notices about you.

Your child has learned of your repressed traits and hidden beliefs through these communication methods. Your responses to situations when you are struggling with a belief or trait tell your child to focus in on your body language, facial expression, and energy. Something important is going on with you and they learn about your repressed traits and beliefs in this way.

Your conscious mind is often unaware of your internal, unconscious struggle, but your energy, eyes, breathing, and body tell your child a different story. Gamblers call these 'tells' because they tell them when the other player is bluffing. This is the very same mechanism by which your child has learned of your hidden and repressed traits and beliefs. Ultimately, your child is unaware that they are learning these things. All they know is that they found another button. Subtle hints are unconsciously given by you every day of your life, and they tell your child if you are happy, in a bad mood, or hiding a repressed trait. In turn, your child will probe and poke you. When you react, you are triggered, and your child will have then confirmed another button.

These behaviors are all very typical, everyday interactions between parent and child. They are unconscious behaviors that neither of you is fully aware of beyond the angst associated with being triggered. As unconscious behaviors, you are unaware of them and are, therefore, unable to control them. This is why there is nothing you could have done to parent your child differently. You were blind, unaware, and powerless to do anything other than, be you. You could not have changed a thing.

It is not just you that your child has observed and can manipulate. Your child will manipulate both parents and, at times, will pit you against each other. This manipulation is a learned behavior that takes advantage of your child's keen knowledge of you both. You are easy victims falling for your child's manipulations almost every time because he knows which of your buttons to push to cause the reaction he wants. It is as if your child has decoded you both into a keyboard of triggers that he can play at will. In some ways, he knows you better than you know yourself.

As our children grow, they amaze us with their capabilities, and they trigger us with their failings. Interestingly, some failings affect only one parent, while others trigger both. In either case, these failings are a gift our children have given to us, and we have given to them.

Yes, you read that last sentence correctly; they are a gift. I understand it does not seem logical or even desirable. But it is, I promise you. It will make sense later when we discuss the fact that triggers are failings shared between you and your child. We will also see that triggers open a doorway into your unconscious mind. A doorway you cannot see until your child shows it to you through those shared triggers. Once the doorway is open, you will see parts of you that have been hidden and repressed for decades. Your journey of self-discovery and self-awareness begins in earnest when you walk through that doorway. I am forever grateful I opened that door and pursued my journey. I hope you will as well.

I have used the term 'trigger' multiple times, and I want you to understand what I mean by that term. Triggers describe our state of being when we have a strong, uncontrolled emotional or physical reaction to something or someone. When triggered, our response is immediate, without thought, and uncontrollable. Our unconscious mind jumps into action and takes command of our conscious thoughts and actions. Something from our past has been awakened, igniting a strong response in us. We are aware of it only in the form of anger, fear, sadness, confusion, irritation, and even rage. These igniting agents are critical to our ability to learn about ourselves. Later in the book, we will discuss methods for using our triggers to analyze our unconscious mind in order to discover who we are and how we define ourselves.

Triggers can be trauma-based or non-trauma-based. Trauma-based triggers, which develop from abuse and other traumatic events, are not the subject of this book. If you have unfortunately suffered from significant traumatic events or abuse, please attempt to differentiate between the two and only work with non-traumatic triggers. If you cannot shut out the trauma-based triggers, you may want to consider putting the book aside until you are ready and able to differentiate between the two.

This book focuses on identifying and healing the inner wounds that are the source of your triggers so that you can become aware of the thoughts and behaviors that have influenced your life's decisions. Triggers are an important phenomenon that we will discuss in detail throughout the book. We will see that hidden, repressed thoughts and beliefs become visible to us through triggers, and we will use this mechanism as a tool in our quest to understand ourselves and our children.

We understand triggering reactions to be very personal and believe they have no impact on others. But this is not true. In later chapters, we will see that our triggers also have a simultaneous effect on our children's lives. This book's focus is on identifying and healing your triggers so that you can become aware of the thoughts and behaviors that have influenced your life's decisions and have contributed to your child's unacceptable behaviors.

Previously, I said your child had decoded you into a keyboard of triggers. By that, I mean that your child can predict how you will respond to your triggers even though your child probably does not know what underlying thing was ignited from your past. Later in the book, when we discuss triggers in more detail, we will see that these igniting agents are critical to our ability to learn about ourselves. We will discuss methods for using our triggers to analyze our unconscious in order to discover who we are and how we define ourselves.

Finally, you will be triggered as you read this book. It could be something I say, or it could be a memory from your past. Please jot down these triggers as they happen, I implore you. These triggers are portals into the inner you. If it was something I said, write down the words exactly. If it was a memory, describe it in detail. After you write down the trigger, describe how you feel and why. Please do not judge or analyze the trigger or your feelings. We only want the facts so that we can explore them later. If images or individual words popped into your head, capture them as well. They may seem random, but they are actually quite valuable.

Please spend the time to journal your triggers; you will be glad you did. Writing them down will probably be both upsetting and quite revealing. Don't forget to honor your feelings, and don't hesitate to meditate to help calm your soul.

Step 1: It's All About You

"Your life is the fruit of your own doing."

Joseph Campbell

The first step in our process toward healing is the most important because it requires you to acknowledge that it is all about you. You are the focal point, and you hold the key to unlock the unconditional love that will heal you and heal the relationship you have with your child. That means change resides within you, first and foremost.

I know that the prospect of fundamental change can be daunting, to say the least. I am sure you are asking yourself what exactly needs to change. At this point in the process, nothing. You don't need to do a thing. Change will occur within you as a natural consequence of self-discovery. All you need to do for this first step is to recognize that change will occur, and believe that it will be for the better. Just commit yourself to a journey of self-discovery, and then let it happen.

Committing yourself to this journey means you have accepted your role as the central figure or main character in your life. It also means this journey is all about you; no one else but you. As such, you are taking responsibility for all aspects of your life. The past, present, and future; the good and the bad.

For some parents, especially mothers, the notion of becoming the focal point of their lives is something they cannot begin to accept. With the birth of their child, they sometimes feel as if they don't exist anymore. Self-imposed and societal expectations demand that the needs of their child come first. Every decision they make everything they do is in service to their child. How can they entertain the notion of becoming the focal point while at the same time be a good parent?

Becoming the focal point of your life is not about asking you to change your priorities and become first in your never-ending list of responsibilities. Nor is it about changing how you rear your child, not in the least. It is about taking ownership of your decisions; however, they are formulated. When you decide to prioritize your child's needs, you should own that decision. Don't use it as an excuse or as a reason why something else went wrong. You decided to prioritize your child because it was the right thing to do even though you knew something else would not be attended to. You made the decision consciously and knowingly after weighing the priorities and needs of everything you are juggling as a parent. Making these decisions in a mindful way like this is critical. Owning them will protect you from building a reservoir of resentment toward your spouse and child.

When you consciously acknowledge ownership of a decision in this way, you will re-evaluate its relative priority; this is good. Your choices will not be automatic and unconscious. You will weigh the implications of your choices against your needs and decide accordingly. Later in the book, we will discuss using mindfulness as a technique for conscious decision-making and awareness.

Let's pause for a moment and think about what it means when you take responsibility for your life. It means you now recognize that you will no longer be able to blame others for your misfortunes. This is not a throw-away statement. It is a fundamental concept that further defines what it means to be responsible for all aspects of your life. One of the problems with blame is that it allows you to transfer responsibility for something to someone else so that you can walk away from the problem. When you do that, you are giving up your power. You are expecting another person to fix the problem. If that problem affects you, then you become dependent upon someone else to fix you, and you are, therefore, dependent upon them for your emotional state. That is very self-defeating and disempowering.

Ultimately, taking responsibility for your life includes taking ownership of your emotional state.

Now I would like you to think about the people and circumstances in your life that are not the way you want them to be. A situation in your life that upsets you, and someone else is to blame for it. Stop for a moment and really think about a specific situation. Who is that person: your mother, spouse, boss, co-worker, or friend? Do you want them to be responsible for your emotional well-being? Is that really what you want? Taking responsibility means that you will no longer be dependent upon others for your happiness and contentment.

For some of you, the idea of being dependent upon someone else for your emotional state is repugnant. For others, the prospect of severing the ties of dependency on that other person will be frightening. Which of these are you? Are you frightened of taking control of your own life? Why? Does the idea of being emotionally dependent upset you? Do you know why you are that way?

Taking responsibility for your life is a critical and fundamental concept that is the basis of any journey of self-discovery. You are responsible for the life you have lived. You ultimately made all of your life decisions, and therefore you are acknowledging your corresponding role and responsibility. As such, there is no one else to blame, nor should there be.

I am certain some of you are sitting there right now feeling guilty and ashamed because you realize this means you are indeed to blame for some of your family's problems. Well, yes and no. Yes, you are responsible for all those decisions. No, you are not an inadequate, incompetent, or unworthy person because of those decisions. I am absolutely certain you made each and every decision based on your assessments of the needs of your family and yourself at that point in time. You made the best decisions you could as you weighed the limitations of time, money, exhaustion, and help. Where is the blame in that?

I suspect some of you might be feeling a little bit anxious

right now. That is OK. Honor those feelings, and write them down. There is probably a trigger hidden in there. If you need to do a Love and Life Meditation, go ahead. I am happy to wait for you.

Not blaming others while taking responsibility for your life is not easy. Typically, whenever we are triggered, or when something irritates us, frustrates us, or throws us into a fit of rage, we look externally and target the person that has triggered us. We think: 'that person is responsible for my response because they triggered me.' This is a normal reaction that we are all guilty of. But, at the same time, we never stop and ask any relevant questions about the situation in order to give us insight into what is happening. Questions such as; what did I do to contribute to the problem? What am I ignoring or protecting by shining the light away from me and on to someone else? What is within me that causes me to react this way? What am I afraid of? What am I hiding? What am I ashamed of? What am I avoiding and not confronting? What was my role?

We don't ask these questions because we don't want to know the answers. It is easier to pass the responsibility on to someone else instead. The majority of us have spent our entire lives dealing with things in this way and have never looked within. We look for something else to be the reason for our discomfort, and we expect others to fix it for us.

When we expect others to fix our problems, we live in a very egocentric world that positions us as the victim and prohibits us from seeing things as they are. When we are blinded in this way, it is nearly impossible to take responsibility for our lives because we have given control of our lives to others. Someone else is responsible for our misfortune, and we don't know the how or why of it. We are ignorant of the real cause and the cure. We only know that it is all happening to us as we sit contently in our blind ignorance as the victim. In this egocentric world, there is no resolution, and it is not possible to become self-aware. Turmoil, chaos, and unhappiness prosper.

If, on the other hand, we choose to ask those questions, then we must be ready to confront the fear, shame, blame, and guilt that will result from the answers. That is not an easy thing to do. So we find ourselves asking if we truly want to be blind and lost, or do we want to see and be found like the verse in John Newton's hymn, 'Amazing Grace' asks?

Pursuing a journey of self-discovery and confronting the truth takes will, courage, and strength. It is a sole endeavor that only you can take alone, not with or for someone else. You have to be mindful and consciously make the choice to face your reality and own your life. A choice, I believe, gives birth to a life of grace, peace, and contentment.

Taking responsibility and owning your life to the fullest is not about blaming others, or yourself for that matter. It is about empowering yourself so that you can take action and remedy the situation. It requires you to be honest and completely vulnerable with yourself. Honesty, and vulnerability, along with courage and strength, are not only prerequisites to undertaking a journey of self-discovery, they are the framework of self-discovery. Think of them as the structure in which self-discovery occurs.

When you take responsibility for your life, you also take ownership of all of the unsavory things you have done or thoughts you have had. My hope is that you can do this with an open heart, empathy, forgiveness, and unconditional love for yourself and others. Yes, this is frightening, but you can do it. The simple fact that you are reading these words tells me you can.

In this chapter, I asked you to stop blaming others and take full responsibility and ownership of your life. I honestly don't believe there is an alternative course of action. When you do not take ownership of your thoughts and words, you deny your reality. When you deny your reality, you deny yourself, and when you deny yourself, you are inconsequential. And, to make matters worse, you are not the only person whose reality is being denied. When you blame others, you threaten their ability to take ownership of their reality because they are charged with yours.

There are two parts to my request to take ownership of your life and stop blaming others. The first part deals with the acknowledgment of the problem. It requires you to objectively see the situation and then clearly define the problem and its impact on you so that you are empowered to pursue a resolution. The second part requires you to let go of blame because it does not do anything to resolve the situation, nor does it help you grow or heal.

Taking responsibility leads you to look within to identify that part of you that contributed to the outcome. It is easy to identify your contribution when the results are good and not so easy when they are undesirable. Identifying that part of you that contributed to the negative outcome will give you insight into your unconscious mind.

As I have said before, this is not an easy subject to pursue because it requires extraordinary courage, honesty, and strength. Whenever you begin to feel overwhelmed or discouraged, I recommend that you envision the beautiful future we discussed earlier and also take a moment and do the Love and Life meditation.

You may also want to watch a TED talk about the importance of confronting your emotional reality. Susan David, Ph.D., a Harvard University researcher, espouses the notion that we should face difficult thoughts, behaviors, and emotions willingly, with curiosity and kindness rather than ignore them. In this way, we will be able to better cope with the realities of life and ultimately be happier, have more meaningful relationships, and be more successful. If you can, please watch Susan David's TED talk 'The Gift and Power of Emotional Courage,' where she discusses these ideas. The link to this TED talk is here:

https://www.ted.com/talks/susan_david_the_gift_and_power_of_emotional_courage?utm_campaign=tedspread&utm_medium=referral&utm_source=tedcomshare

Before moving on to the next chapter, I'd like to discuss courage, the prerequisite virtue needed to undertake a journey of self-discovery. The vast majority of people never undertake a journey of self-discovery because they live in an unconscious state and are unaware of the possibility. For those of us who are aware, we don't pursue it because it is both frightening and daunting. Yet we have a great interest in other people's pursuit of self-discovery and will read stories or watch movies about people who undertake epic journeys of this kind.

The Hero's Journey is a literary genre that is all about self-discovery. 'Harry Potter and the Philosopher's Stone,' 'The Lion King,' 'Star Wars,' and 'The Odyssey' are all examples of the Hero's Journey. It is one of the oldest forms of storytelling, and it was popularized in our modern culture by Joseph Campbell. The Hero's Journey tells the story of a person who goes on a difficult, and at times terrifying, adventure. They are confronted with an overwhelming crisis that they must overcome. When they return home, they are a better, wiser, and more complete person. The journey is a genuinely transformative experience for the hero because he learns who he is and what is ultimately important to him in his life. In each of these stories, the protagonist exhibits extraordinary courage even though they have significant doubts about themselves. They often do not believe they have what it takes to complete their journey. But in the end, they find the courage deep within their soul.

For me, a journey of self-discovery is also a Hero's Journey. It takes lots of courage, but in the end, you will return transformed into a better person who knows without a doubt, who you are, and what is important in your life. As Joseph Campbell once said, "You are the hero of your own Story."

What is stopping you from pursuing your hero's journey?

Step 2: A Journey Through Shadows

"How can I be substantial if I do not cast a shadow?"

Carl Jung

If the first step is to take full responsibility for your life and stop looking externally to blame others, then the second step is to recognize that there are parts of you that you are entirely unaware of. Said differently, you possess personality traits and beliefs that you have so thoroughly repressed that you do not know you have them. You are blind to their very existence. These traits and beliefs are buried deep within your unconscious mind and are invisible to you because you have unknowingly rejected them as yours even though they are a part of you. Your unconscious mind has rejected these traits and beliefs because they are perceived as being inferior, repugnant, or unacceptable in some way.

Some of you have reread that last paragraph multiple times because it does not make logical sense. How can a person reject something they don't know exists? If it does not exist, how can you evaluate it and determine if it is inferior, repugnant, or unacceptable? How can that be?

The key to understanding this is to understand the unconscious mind. Our mind has the remarkable ability to take a known thing, such as a memory, and hide it from us. It buries those memories within the section of our mind that we call the unconscious. The memories stored in our unconscious mind are effectively lost and forgotten and are referred to as being 'repressed'. The extraordinary thing about the unconscious mind is that those memories are not actually lost or forgotten. They are there. They are stored in the deep recesses of our brain like an archive file on a computer. It is not until we 'un-archive' the memory and move it from the unconscious section of our mind to the conscious section that it becomes remembered and known to us again.

The process of burying memories into our unconscious mind occurs after we have determined that those thoughts and beliefs are too painful to keep alive in our conscious mind. This process usually happens instantaneously without us being aware of it.

In addition to memories, the unconscious mind can also repress thoughts, beliefs, and personality traits. Another term used to describe all repressed things is 'disowned'. The process of burying our painful memories and disowned traits is a powerful coping mechanism we all benefit from. It is not an abnormality that inflicts some of us and not others. It is a normal, healthy function of the unconscious mind that protects us from confronting emotionally painful realities.

This facility to repress and disown things as a means of protection is extraordinarily effective and thorough. I can't tell you the number of times I have spoken to people about their disowned and repressed traits only to find that they have completely forgotten the details of the discussion minutes later. These are discussions where I have specifically called their attention to the fact that we discussed one of their disowned traits. I would get them to acknowledge the disowned trait as theirs and have them expand upon its characteristics. Then, 10 minutes later, they would have no memory of the repressed trait. They would remember that we had a conversation. They would remember me asking if they realized we were talking about their disowned traits. But, they would be unable to recall any of the details of the specific trait. It was as if someone purposefully zapped their disowned trait from their brain.

This forgetfulness has happened to me; many times, in fact. I am sure it will happen again when I touch upon something particularly painful. It amazes me every time it happens. It isn't easy to imagine or understand until you see it occur or have it happen to you. Trust me; it is a real thing. I suspect there is a standard psychological term for this phenomenon, but I call it emotional blindness.

This forgetfulness will happen to you as we work our way through this book. That is why I want you to write things down. We will be going through different processes and techniques where it will be vital for you to remember details. When we do, I will ask you to take notes. Please be ready. I strongly suggest you jot down your thoughts as they happen. I am not at all suggesting formal note-taking, although doing that is OK. I am recommending that you jot down anything, including random thoughts and images, as they happen, without filter or constraint. Joseph Campbell, the American mythologist, described the importance of this request when he said, "When your heart speaks, take good notes."

As I stated at the beginning of this chapter, the second step in our self-discovery process is to recognize that we are entirely unaware of parts of ourselves. It is very difficult for most people to understand or accept this fact. The vast majority of people believe they have complete knowledge of themselves and can't fathom the contrary notion that they have disowned and repressed parts of themselves. They reject the idea that they do not know every little bit there is to know about themselves. Yet, they can easily see this very same willful blindness in others.

The phrase 'look who is calling the kettle black' or 'the pot calling the kettle black' is an excellent example of not being able to see our repressed traits. It is an idiom of the English language that describes someone who criticizes another person for a fault that they also have. This idiom illustrates how easy it is to recognize when someone else is blind and cannot see their own similar 'negative' personality traits. Personality traits that they have repressed and disowned.

But the fact remains that this idiom is true for you and for me as well.

The personality traits and beliefs that we cannot see are a normal phenomenon of the human psyche. In psychological study, they are referred to as 'Alter Ego,' 'Id,' 'Disowned Self,' and 'Shadow.' The story of Dr. Jekyll and Mr. Hyde is a well-known reflection of this concept.

Carl Jung, the Swiss psychiatrist who founded analytical psychology, introduced the world to the concept of shadows. Jung defined shadows as the traits and beliefs that we reject, dislike, or would rather ignore. He saw them as an integral part of the larger unconscious mind. According to Jung, the unconscious is "... everything of which I was once conscious but have now forgotten; everything perceived by my senses, but not noted by my conscious mind; everything which, involuntarily and without paying attention to it, I feel, think, remember, want and do; all the future things which are taking shape in me and will sometime come to consciousness; all this is the content of the unconscious... Besides these, we must include all more or less intentional repressions of painful thoughts and feelings."

Shadows reside within our unconscious mind and are seeded from both primitive, evolutionary sources as well as our personal life experiences. Our basic instincts, such as procreation, preservation, and aggression, are sources for some of our shadows. But most of our shadows are sourced from our parents, teachers, and siblings when they responded harshly to us with rejection, anger, fear, anxiety, punishment, or criticism.

I want to restate this last point because it will become important when we discuss the process of finding our own shadows. Specifically, some of our shadows result from contemptuous interactions with our caregivers during early childhood that have damaged us in a significant way. Parents, teachers, and siblings who love us would never want to consciously hurt us with scornful rejection, anger, fear, anxiety, punishment, or criticism, but unfortunately, they do. It happens all too often, even though we wish it did not. Sometimes, when we lose our composure when dealing with a child, we inadvertently plant a shadow seed into that child's unconscious mind that scars them for life. I have unfortunately done it to my children. We are imperfect human beings.

Other factors also contribute to the content of our shadows. Societal norms and family tenets frame the boundaries of what is acceptable to us and our communities. The traits, beliefs, and behaviors that live outside these boundaries are viewed as shameful, odd, repugnant, objectionable, and undesirable. As such, they also spur the creation of shadows.

Some shadows are multi-generational passing from parent to child. The opening of this book describes a multi-generational shadow between me, my mother, and my daughter. To illustrate this, I'd like you to think back to the last large family gathering you attended. Have you ever wondered why so many of your extended family members exhibit the very same behaviors, especially the cringe-worthy ones? Have you noticed there are a few family members who are so repulsed by those common family traits that they have become anti-zealots doing the exact opposite? These are most likely shadows that have been passed down to subsequent generations.

The process of passing shadows down to the next generation is insidious. Later in the book, I will walk you through the details of the memory of me realizing I messed up my daughter. The experience was both heart-wrenching and profound. Even so, I am very grateful that I had the experience and figured it out for two reasons. The first reason is that I could share it with my daughter. That will allow her to incorporate it into her journey of self-awareness. When she does, it won't be passed on to the next generation. The second reason is that I could see the impact of this shadow on my mother and empathize with her plight. This new understanding formed the basis from which I could finally forgive my mother.

In summary, our shadows are usually seeded during our childhood from many sources. They are repressed and hidden deep within the jail of our unconscious mind. Our shadows are locked in by the bars of guilt, shame, and blame. They are kept there, in our unconscious, suppressed and concealed from everyone, including ourselves.

Finally, I'd like to share a little wisdom from my grandmother. When I was about 20 years old and felt a bit overwhelmed by my life, my grandmother told me that I had to "Kiss it up to God." Then she kissed her two fingers and flung the kiss up toward heaven. Needless to say, I rolled my eyes and continued to worry about my life.

My grandmother was a very practical, no-nonsense Italian woman with a third-grade education. Although she did not speak English very well, she expressed complex subjects in straightforward terms. Eventually, I realized she was telling me that there are times in your life when you have to let go and have faith that things will be OK. The act of kissing your woes up to God was not about ignoring them or throwing them away. It was about having them held in a safe place to explore later when you are ready to face them. Your mind will protect you from confronting things you are not yet ready to handle. Please be patient with yourself. You will eventually remember the 'archived' events of your life. All you need to do is let it happen. Memories will come to the forefront of your mind the way they did for me[1]. Time is on your side.

Earlier, I asked you to accept responsibility for your life and to do so without the cover of blame. In this chapter, I have told you about the traits and beliefs you possess but have repressed. You have hidden them within your unconscious mind because they are too painful to bear. This is a frightening thought, and it may be one of those times when you need to have faith that you can and will be able to address those things at a later date. If so, please follow my grandmother's guidance and kiss your fear, anger, guilt, or resentment up to God for safekeeping.

---

[1] I describe this process in my book 'The Inconsequential Child'

Shadows Are Not Good Or Bad

*"Anyone who perceives his shadow, and his light
simultaneously sees himself from two sides, and thus gets
in the middle."*

Carl Jung

In addition to shadows, Jung introduced us to the concept of archetypes. Archetypes are the different types of people or characters that are known by everyone across cultures and time. For example, when I say the word 'king', you instantly conjure up an image in your mind of a king complete with a specific wardrobe, a detailed understanding of their personality, how they stand and hold themselves, and even their energy. Furthermore, if you were to make a painting of that king and show it to anyone, anywhere in the world, they would instantly recognize it as a picture of a king.

Archetypes possess very specific qualities and traits that reflect the best and worst characteristics of that type of person. The ideal king, for instance, would exhibit the attributes of a courageous, benevolent, and wise leader. On the other hand, there is an equal and opposite set of characteristics that describe the worst possible king, namely, a tyrannical despot. Kings can be weak or strong, tyrannical or benevolent. Imagine living in a kingdom ruled by a tyrant as opposed to a compassionate, wise leader; not a very pleasant thought. A reality you can imagine because you are familiar with the archetype of a tyrannical king.

In the story of the Lion King, Simba's uncle, Scar, is an example of the weak tyrant king. Scar is in contrast to Simba's father, Mufasa, who is a courageous, wise, and benevolent leader. I will use the characters of Mufasa and Scar in this chapter to illustrate archetypes and their corresponding shadows.

Jung's archetypes and shadows are tightly coupled. If we looked at the personality traits of the King archetype from the perspective of shadows, we would see that Mufasa and Scar are shadows of each other. Neither of them would ever want to be the type of king the other exemplifies. As such, Mufasa would repress and hide the traits and beliefs that would make him a tyrant, while Scar would never let his subjects see him as benevolent. Scar wants everyone to fear him. He rules through intimidation.

As we can see by contrasting Scar and Mufasa, not all shadow traits are negative or 'bad'. Scar's shadows are the traits and beliefs we typically think of as 'good'. Being a benevolent king is a good thing. But for Scar, it is not. He believes being benevolent is a weakness. This belief is therefore one of Scar's shadow traits.

Unfortunately, it is common for people to think about shadows as being bad, dark, or evil when, in reality, they are neither good nor bad. They are simply disowned and rejected.

For every disowned shadow trait, there is an equally powerful yet opposite trait; we call that its antithesis. I think of the 'positive' and 'negative' traits of shadows as being equal but opposite, like the north and south poles of a magnet. One person may have a shadow trait sourced from the north pole of the magnet while another person may have that same shadow sourced from the south pole. Mufasa and Scar exemplify this dichotomy because they possess shadows that are the antithesis of each other. Neither pole is good or bad, they are simply opposites.

With this magnet analogy, the magnetic energy is the shadow. The traits can be expressed at either end of the magnetic field. The north and south poles are the opposites. One end is repressed and is referred to as your shadow; the other end is not. That is why I believe labeling shadows as being 'good' or 'bad' is not helpful. 'Goodness' and 'badness' do not accurately reflect the characteristics of the shadow.

The key concept to remember is that the repressed and disowned traits of a shadow have an equal but opposite set of traits and beliefs that are alive within us. The repressed and disowned shadow traits reside deep within our unconscious, and they will impact the decisions we make and the life we live in many different ways. Shadows are not good or bad; they are disowned, rejected and hidden from our conscious selves.

At this point in our discussion, I would not be surprised if you are wondering what the difference is between shadow traits and personality traits. It is a reasonable question to ask, and as we will see, this difference is quite important to understand.

I think of shadow traits as describing who you are at a fundamental, essential level. Shadow traits define your identity in terms of your morals, values, and beliefs. To give you an idea of how we define ourselves, and each other, I'd like you to think of a friend, brother, or sister. Then in one, or two sentences, tell me about them. Literally, take a moment, and describe your best friend, brother, or sister to me. Please write down your two-sentence description as if you were sending me a text.

The words you used most likely described their morals, values, and beliefs. You probably wrote something like, my friend is a great guy who is kind and honest. You can count on him whenever you need help. The words honest, kind and dependable described his morals, values, and beliefs.

Since the concepts of morals, values, and beliefs are often confused, I'd like to offer the following definitions:

Morals: A person's principles or standards concerning what is and is not acceptable for them to do or believe, i.e., what is right, and what is wrong.

Values: The societal or cultural equivalent of morals. A culture's principles and standards concerning what is good or bad in society. Rugged individualism, religious freedom, separation of church and state, free speech, and capitalism are all examples of US cultural values. As individuals, we decide whether or not to adopt the larger societal values.

Beliefs: The tenets or convictions that a person holds to be true. Within the context of a person's identity, beliefs are the set of morals and values that make up the person's definition of self.

Now I'd like you to reread the description you wrote about your friend or sibling in light of these definitions. Can you see that you described them in terms of morals, values, and beliefs? These are all qualities of their identity which describe who they are at a foundational level. As we progress, we will see that shadows have a fundamental impact on a person's identity.

On the other hand, personality traits are how you act out your identity. They are the outward presentation of your identity in terms of the image you display to others, the behaviors you exhibit, and the things you say. Think back to the friend you just described, and try to remember your favorite story about them. That story will be all about their personality. The story will exemplify or validate one or more of the morals, values, and beliefs you used to describe them.

Another way to illustrate these concepts is to use one of my shadows as an example. Specifically, I have a shadow around being needy. This shadow manifests in me as having an aversion toward dependency on anyone, for anything, for any reason. I do not expect or rely on others for help, comfort, acknowledgment, or compassion.

When I see neediness in an able-body person, I lose respect for that person, and I consciously avoid them at all costs. As a result of this shadow, I became, and still am, a very self-reliant and independent person who is capable and competent in many ways. I am one of those people who can do almost anything. I have taught myself many things, and I do most things alone, rarely if ever asking others for help.

I developed this shadow around neediness in direct response

to what I did not have during my childhood. The things I needed as a child were emotional attachment, comfort, and acknowledgment. But my shadow manifested in the opposite form of neediness, i.e., independence and self-reliance, which is the antithesis of neediness. I disowned the need for emotional attachment and, therefore, disowned being needy. Thus, my identity is defined as being independent and self-reliant, both emotionally and functionally. I value competent, capable, strong people and have little regard for needy people.

This disregard for needy people and the fact that I don't respect them is what my daughter knew about me, and it is the reason why she would not come to me for help.

My personality is expressed in my behaviors, which are to avoid needy people whenever possible. I do not tolerate people who whine, cry, or complain. 'Stop being a baby' and 'suck it up' were common retorts in my life. Prior to my wife, I dated women who did not trigger my needy antibodies. They were self-centered and not compassionate, and I, in turn, never allowed them to give me comfort. How does one love and form healthy relationships with this point of view and corresponding behaviors?

As you can see, my identity centers around independence. This trait is in direct response to my neediness shadow, but it manifested as its opposite, i.e., being self-reliant instead of dependent. My behaviors and personality support my independence in various ways, including my attitudes and responses to needy people. These behaviors make me appear uncaring and dismissive of specific types of people.

In summary, shadows are neither good nor bad, and they are expressed either as is or as its opposite. Please recall the magnet analogy where shadows are the magnetic field, and we manifest our shadows at either the north or south poles. Our identity is expressed in terms of the morals, values, and beliefs that define us, while our personality is expressed through the things we say and do in support of our identity.

Step 3: An Unknown Life

*"Until you make the unconscious conscious, it will direct
your life, and you will call it fate."*

Carl Jung

The third step in our process is to recognize that your
unconscious mind has controlled substantial portions of your
life. Said differently, your shadows have directed many of
your life's decisions and have had an invisible yet significant
influence over you and the life you have lived.

Accepting this is both disturbing and humbling because it
means you have not been in control of your life. It also means
that your conscious mind is not as powerful as you believe
it to be, and your unconscious mind is not at all passive. On
the contrary, your unconscious mind, and your shadows
specifically, have not only molded your identity in ways that
are currently invisible to you, they have also had a say in most
of your life's decisions.

Your unconscious mind is quite powerful. It is capable of
regularly biasing the way you interpret reality, and it has directly
guided every decision you have ever made. Knowledge of this
fact is critical to understanding how you define yourself and
how you interact with the world around you. It also explains
why shadows have such power over us.

For this book's purpose, the important concept to remember
is that our identity and self-image are heavily influenced, if not
directly defined, by our shadows. Our shadows also influence
our interactions with others so that we can maintain harmony
and consistency with our definition of self[2]. In other words, our

---

2 These conclusions are somewhat based on Freud's concept of the Ego
which he defined as the conscious awareness of 'self' and the place where we

behaviors toward others reflect our identity, and our identity is defined within the context of our shadows.

Let me unpack that last sentence a bit. Our identity defines who we are and how we live and interact in the world. For instance, a person who sees themselves as a victim will interact with others very differently than someone who does not define themselves in that way. Our self-identity is based on our core thoughts and beliefs; we are who we think we are. Our conscious thoughts and beliefs form the mask that we project out to the world, and then there are our fears and doubts, which form and mold the mask. Those fears and doubts are sourced from our shadows which reside in our unconscious mind.

Our shadows are ever-present and do not eventually disappear over time. They live in our unconscious mind and come to life in a variety of conscious forms, sometimes wreaking havoc in our lives. They have the means to control our thoughts, emotions, and behaviors, and they may even drive us toward unhealthy choices and challenging times. We are so utterly blinded from the reality of our unconscious mind that we are ignorant of the fact that some of our problems are often self-imposed and not the result of luck or circumstance. Jung emphasizes this concept with the quote at the top of this chapter. He also said, "That which we do not bring to consciousness appears in our lives as fate.

A common example of someone whose problems are self-imposed and controlled by their unconscious mind are those people who get involved in the same type of unhealthy relationship again and again. These people convince themselves it will be different each and every time because their new

---

establish our identity. The Ego acts as the arbitrator between our conscious mind and the different aspects of unconscious minds i.e., the Id and the Super-ego. Jung extended the definition of Ego to include that part of the psyche where we have a sense of existence. The Ego links our inner and outer worlds together, forming our self-image and regulating how we relate to the external world including our relationships with others.

romantic interest is nothing like the last. For you, the observer, it is evident that this person is again headed for disaster. It is clear to you that they are incapable of seeing things as they really are.

It is also quite baffling to you that they can delude themselves into believing a false reality as they continue to repeat the same pattern of unhealthy decision-making. If you know this person well enough to discuss their relationships with them, they will describe the hurt, anger, sadness, and fear they feel. This description of their pain will be genuine and based on truthful reality. They will tell you that they honestly do not want to be in an unhealthy relationship, and they indeed do not. Their conscious mind knows this without confusion or conflict. They absolutely do not want to make the same mistake. Yet they repeat the pattern and do it again and again. Why? Because their unconscious mind is so much more powerful. They blame their relationship problems on their partner's flaws and inadequacies rather than on their shadows. It would take extreme courage for them to become vulnerable enough with themselves to do the kind of self-reflection necessary to uncover the actual reasons why they get into the same unhealthy relationships.

Then there are people with addictions or self-destructive behaviors. They struggle with these behaviors despite consciously knowing that they would be better off not engaging in them. They are often powerless to control themselves and are tortured by their addiction's damaging and unhealthy effects. Addicts frequently tell themselves they will kick the habit and live a clean life. And then, before they know it, their shadow takes over, and they seek out the next hit[3]. How is it that they engage in these acts when they know they will later feel shame, guilt, fear, and sadness in addition to the unhealthy effects of the addiction?

---

3 Please note that I am not trivializing the powerful chemical and emotional effect of addiction. That reality makes things that much more difficult.

These two examples illustrate the influence shadows have over the conscious decisions we make as well as our expectations, assessments, and desires. In the case of the person who repeatedly gets involved in unhealthy relationships, they are attracted to people who fulfill an unknown need. The need is unknown to them because it has been repressed and is hidden within their unconscious mind. It is a need that was sourced from one of their shadows. The remarkable thing about this need and their behavior is that they consistently choose partners who are adept at fulfilling that need. They do this even though they are unable to describe the need because it is unknown to them. It is a disowned, repressed shadow need. Since it is a shadow need, the relationship devolves into a disastrous affair of conflict and pain. The same is true for the addict, except the addict fulfills his need via a substance or behavior rather than a person.

There are two parts to the shadow play described in these examples. The first is utter blindness. I find it amazing to see exactly how powerful the human mind is as it protects us with this blindness. You can clearly see the pattern of behavior being repeated, but the person who is getting into another unhealthy relationship cannot see a thing. They have a need that is somehow fulfilled by the unhealthy partner even though they are utterly oblivious to their need. The second part has to do with the specifics of the shadow itself. That shadow, and the corresponding need fulfillment, is what causes the disastrous result.

These are two examples of the unconscious mind's power to control our behaviors. The unconscious control that our shadow can exert upon us is immense, even if we are unaware of the role our shadows play. The psychological mechanisms at play are fascinating, but we will not discuss them here because the topic is beyond the scope of this book. However, the critical thing to know is that these unhealthy behaviors are manifestations of our personal, unconscious struggle with our shadows. We are all directly affected by them, whether we realize it or not.

A person's shadows do indeed direct the conscious mind to construct a false reality along with behaviors and decisions appropriate for that reality. In the example of the person who repeatedly chooses the wrong lover, they live in a false reality because they honestly believe their new partner is different from the others. Their focus is on their partner's character rather than the reasons why they chose them as their partner. They have no idea what motivated them to make the decisions they made.

The false reality and corresponding behaviors are a construct of our unconscious mind, and we are at its mercy until we become aware of its power and can see our shadows. Only then can we gain control and effect beneficial change.

The impact of shadow on life's decisions is comprehensive. It impacts the career you choose, the jobs you pursue, your clothes, your friendships, and who you marry. As I mentioned earlier, my 'needy' shadow led me to become fiercely independent. I was that way all my life. When I graduated from college, I had an opportunity to interview at IBM, one of the premier high-tech companies at the time; this was a dream opportunity.

IBM had a very rigid ethos and a strict dress code, so I bought a suit and shaved off my beard. I flew to White Plains, NY, where I spent my first night ever in a hotel. I was scheduled for interviews with seven people the next day. After the 3rd interview, I stopped the process and left because I was shocked at everything I saw. The most disturbing was the hundreds of employees dressed in the same blue suit. I realized I could never assimilate into their culture and conform to their rules. My need to be independent would not fly at IBM.

At the time, I was completely unaware of shadows, but I was very aware that I felt uncomfortable and anxious while I was there. It was clear to me that their expectations were incompatible with mine. The aversion was so great that I walked away from my dream career without hesitation. Only now, in hindsight, do I understand the shadow dance that was at play.

Step 4: Mirror, Mirror

*"Knowing your own darkness is the best method for
dealing with the darknesses of other people."*

Carl Jung

We just discussed the third step along our path to self-awareness, which is to accept the fact that our unconscious mind, and shadows, in particular, have a significant impact on our daily lives. We saw how our current life condition, our job, where we live, how we live, and our beliefs could all be traced back to our shadow traits. An investigation of our lives, with an understanding of how our unconscious mind works, will clearly show that the life we lead is actually a reflection of our shadows. Our life is a manifestation of our unconscious mind and our shadows in particular.

The next step toward self-awareness is to see our shadows reflected back to us through those we love. Our children, parents, and the people we are close to possess some of our shadows and they, in turn, reflect them back to us. A phenomenon we are often entirely unaware of. We frequently have no idea that our loved ones carry our shadow traits and beliefs, nor do we realize they are mirroring them back for us to see.

There are two types of shadow material that your child holds for you; the things he sees in you that he finds abhorrent and therefore rejects and the things he has unknowingly adopted as his own. In other words, your child has adopted some of your shadows in the same way you have and he has taken on other shadows in their antithesis form.

Recall the magnet analogy where the shadow is expressed from either the north or south pole. Your child will internalize some of your shadow traits in either of the two-pole forms.

You may exhibit that shadow trait from the north pole while your child will exhibit his version from the south pole. Do not presume your child's shadows are an exact replica of yours.

It is perfectly normal for your child to incorporate some of your most potent shadows while rejecting others. In either case, your child is mirroring hidden parts of you for you to observe through them. Mirroring your shadows in this way is a gift that you may not yet fully appreciate. Later in the book, we will discuss why it is a gift of significant value. But for now, you need to be able to see your child's shadows and acknowledge them as reflections of you so that you can begin your journey toward acceptance, integration, and self-love.

Your child not only possesses your shadows, but they also possess some of their other parent's shadows as well. These two sets of shadows combine with the shadows they have developed over their lifetime to complete the collection of shadows that make your child unique.

'Oh my God, she is just like her mother...' or 'the apple doesn't fall far from the tree...' are common phrases we have used to acknowledge the fact that a child has adopted behaviors and traits from their parent. This is very easy for us to see and recognize in others but not as easy to see in ourselves. Parents can usually see this only when the child is doing something 'good', something they hold in high esteem. However, when the child is doing something unacceptable, parents are unable to attribute their child's negative behaviors to themselves. They are often willfully blind to that reality. The degree to which they are blind is directly related to how deeply they have repressed that specific shadow trait.

The very same phenomenon is true for the child. Children will often mimic the thoughts and behaviors of their parents. Children feel pride when their parents praise them for mimicking the thoughts and behaviors their parents hold highly. However, children get angry and resentful when their parents admonish and renounce them for mimicking thoughts and behaviors sourced from their parents' 'negative' shadows. This inconsistency leads the child to confusion because the child does not realize they are mimicking disowned traits and beliefs. Eventually the child concludes that their parents are hypocrites.

Parents are often completely unaware that the negative thoughts and behaviors their child mimics are sourced from them. To illustrate the depth of this blindness, I'd like you to think about a sister, brother, cousin, or close friend who has a child. Think back to a time when you observed heartwarming or positive interactions between that parent and child. Are you able to see just how similar the child is to the parent? Similarities including physical body movements, facial expressions as well as shared interests, thoughts, and beliefs. Do you see their joy and also the depth of the energy they are sharing? A beautiful and amazing thing to watch.

Now think back to a time of conflict between that parent and child. A time when you thought the kid was acting just like their parent, but the parent could not see it. They were oblivious to the fact that their child was mirroring them. You know these times; its when you think to yourself that the parent is finally getting 'a taste of their own medicine'. Did you see a repeating pattern play out between them? A familiar pattern where you could clearly see where the dysfunction was coming from and why.

The parent was utterly oblivious to their role in the triggering as their child was poking them. It is as if an electric wire was attached to the parent shocking them with each interaction. Can you remember the intensity of the energy flowing between the parent and the child? An upsetting yet amazing phenomenon to observe as well.

In both the 'positive' and 'negative' scenarios, you could see your sister, brother, cousin, or friend within their child. You could also see their child mirroring their parent's shadows and triggering them accordingly. As the third-party observer, it was quite apparent to you.

The next time you see this shadow dance play out between a parent and a child, you will watch it with a deeper understanding. You will see it more clearly and will have a way to describe the behavioral patterns that unfold before you. You will be surprised at how obvious it all is and how blind you have been all these years.

Now let's personalize these memories a bit. If you have a child, try to remember the 'good' and the 'bad' interactions you have had with your child. Stop for a moment, and take this time to reflect. Literally, pause from reading and bring both of your hands to your heart and breathe in and out slowly as you hold your heart with unconditional love. Close your eyes and try to remember an interaction with your child; let yourself feel the memory.

If you paused and spent the time to do this, you most likely were flooded with emotion. Maybe you were filled with sadness and remorse. For many of you, no memory came forth. This is because your mind was protecting you. It is a form of emotional blindness, a very real and powerful thing. Please don't fret about it. Be thankful that you know how to protect yourself. Some day soon, you will be able to peak over your wall of emotional blindness and see these things.

If you were able to remember a specific interaction with your child, try to observe that memory impartially. The way you were able to remember the other parent and their interaction with their child. Can you? Can you see yourself being triggered? Can you see yourself in your child? Can you see the shadow your child is reflecting back to you? Can you see the shadow dance? If you can, you may want to journal that memory.

If you are not able to see this, it is OK too. This is a very challenging thing to do. Most people are not able to see themselves or their shadows in this way until they have practice. It requires you to put yourself in the third party observer's position during a time when you are in the middle of an intense, emotional interaction with a loved one. But, as you saw with your sister, brother, cousin, or close friend, the shadow dance between parent and child is a very real phenomenon that is true for you as well.

Some of you may be feeling paternal guilt right now. I want you to know there is no blame or shame here. You are not a horrible, incompetent parent for allowing your children to see and adopt your shadows. It is all so very normal. You are simply a human being coping with your own personal demons, something we all do every day. You have been struggling your whole life with little if any knowledge of the how, what, where, when, and why of your shadows. You have been coping as best you can without the necessary skills to effect meaningful change. Also, please do not forget that you, too, are a child of parents who struggled with their demons, coping as best they could. But now, you know the dance. I want you to know there is hope; change is possible.

Now may be a good time to take a moment for a Love and Life Meditation.

Do either of your parents trigger you? I am confident at least one of them does. If you think about it within the context of this book, you will see that you are the child I have described in this chapter. That means you participated in this shadow dance with your parents in the same way your child has with you. The point I am trying to make is that parents are also children. That puts them in the unique and beneficial position of being able to understand this mirroring phenomenon from both perspectives and can, therefore, glean different insights from each. You may want to re-read this chapter again and place yourself in the position of the child rather than the parent.

Finally, please do not go to your spouse or your children and tell them that you share their same shadows. The reasons for this are twofold. The first is they will not understand. This is a very complex subject, and they don't have the prerequisite knowledge. Also, they will probably interpret it as you blaming them for your problems. They will shut-down and place all sorts of barriers up around this topic. The second reason is that it's too soon. There will be a time and a place to discuss this with your loved ones. But it is not now. We will review this process near the end of the book.

Step 5: Why Do They Trigger Me?

"Everything that irritates us about others can lead us to an understanding of ourselves."

Carl Jung

In the previous chapter, we discussed the fourth step of self-awareness: to see your shadows reflected back to you through those you love, especially your child. The fifth step is to find your shadows by recognizing that the shadows reflected back to you are yours. This step requires you to make the shadow visible and an acknowledged part of your identity. This is probably the most challenging part of the process because it requires you to directly confront realities that have been repressed for the vast majority of your life. However, the benefits of this process are profound, and they begin with unconditional self-love.

In the next few chapters, I will present two different techniques for finding and accepting your shadows. However, in this chapter, we will discuss the shadows we see in others. The term used to describe this phenomenon is projection. Projection is sometimes referred to as blame-shifting. It is an unconscious defense mechanism in which your ego protects itself by attributing something unwanted or emotionally painful to someone else. We do this because it is too painful to acknowledge the projection as our own. For example, a married man who is attracted to another woman might accuse her of flirting with him. Or a bully often projects his feelings of inadequacy onto the person he is bullying.

Jung talked about the concept of projection in the quote at the top of this chapter. Jung believed that we could identify our shadow traits and beliefs by observing the people who trigger us. They trigger us because we have projected our shadows onto them.

Projecting your shadow onto someone else is an unconscious act. It occurs when you see your shadow being acted out by another person, regardless of whether or not your shadow material is indeed true for them. You believe it to be true, and that is what you see. You feel yourself being triggered by that person's behaviors, so you blame them for all sorts of things that may or may not be relevant to them or their motives.

We are utterly incapable of realizing that we are projecting our shadow until we tune into the trigger and make the connection back to ourselves. For instance, that married man who says the woman is flirting with him will pass a lie detector test until he realizes it is his projection that is causing him to believe she is flirting. Ultimately, we see what we want to believe, and we believe what we want to see.

In the early stages of learning about your shadow, you cannot see the shadow being acted out visibly. More precisely, you realize that that person's behavior triggers you, but you don't recognize the source as your shadow. Instead, you feel it in the form of rage, anxiety, fear, or anger. All you know is that you are being triggered, and the trigger is coming from the person who is driving you crazy. You can describe the thing you see them doing, and that is as far as your understanding goes. You don't realize that the triggering is a projection sourced from a wound residing deep within you.

The implications of the last few paragraphs are disturbing because it completely changes the way you have understood and dealt with triggers. Specifically, triggers don't have anything to do with other people's character flaws. Instead, triggers are sourced from you, not them. Your trigger is ignited because you have a painful memory that has left a scar deep within your unconscious mind. That person did something that touched that painful wound, and you are then triggered.

If your child is the person triggering you, then it is possible that your child is indeed manifesting the shadow. This is because children adopt some of their parents' shadows. In that case, you are seeing your shadow in them as they act as a mirror into your unconscious. When I first realized this I was simultaneously stunned and thankful for the gift my children hold for me. Where else could I see the real me?

Regardless of who the triggering person is, the triggering behaviors and thoughts we see in others are more about us than they are about the other person. As you know, one of my shadow behaviors is to avoid needy people because they irritate me beyond belief. I manifest this shadow in its antithesis form, i.e., as a complete rejection of any need. I never seek compassion or comfort from others. When I see neediness in other people, I reject them. What I am actually doing is projecting my neediness onto them, and then I respond to that projection by rejecting and avoiding them at all costs.

Let me explain in detail what is happening... The person who triggers me is doing something that reminds me of a painful memory or event where I needed love, connection, acknowledgment, compassion, understanding, etc. On a conscious level, I am entirely unaware of this memory, its pain, or the need. All I know consciously is that person is needy. My immediate response is to become angry at them and reject them. But subconsciously, I am fully able to see their behavior and make the connection to the painful event from my past. Rather than bring that memory into my consciousness and re-live the pain, my subconscious evokes emotional blindness to protect me from my painful past. At the same time, my conscious mind falls into emotional chaos, and I become triggered.

Having done intense shadow work, I now know that being needy is just as much a part of me as it is a part of the needy people that I avoid. This shadow developed because I was desperately deprived of emotional attachment as a child. Unfortunately, my mother was severely depressed and was unable to provide me with the comfort I needed when I was very young. A few years ago, I wrote a memoir called 'The

Inconsequential Child,' which described the circumstances in which I realized that I was an emotionally neglected child. It took me many years and a lot of work to figure it all out. And, in so doing, I learned of this shadow and how I manifest it.

The people we project our shadows upon are the ones who irritate and anger us. We don't just randomly choose any individual as the target of our projection. The person we select will exhibit a behavior that is related to our shadow in some form. It may be a very slight, trivial expression of the shadow, or that person could openly act out our hidden and repressed traits with wanton disregard. In either case, it does not mean that person has the same shadow.

Although we see our faults and shadows within that person, we are unable to recognize them as our own. All we know is that the person triggers us beyond belief. We then find fault in them and blame them for our emotional response. Our blindness is profound, and our response to it is unhelpful.

We all know that we are not perfect. We have made poor decisions and have done things in the past that we are not proud of. We have addictions and jealousies, we think bad thoughts, and we may even hate some people. We all know that everyone has flaws, but ultimately, when we boil it all down, we are fundamentally good, kind, and loving people trying to do the right thing every day. Even still, the idea that we possess the very same shadows as the person who triggers us threatens our self-image and strains our credulity. It forces us to question how we see ourselves and experience the world. Accepting this reality is often a challenging task.

I want you to consider one other thing about people who trigger us. They are not much different from you and me. As a matter of fact, you and I may be someone else's triggering person. Remember, we are all fundamentally good people trying to do the right thing every day of our lives.

Before I detail the techniques for finding and accepting your shadows, I want you to be ready to take notes. If I were you, the reader, I know that I would simply ignore this request. In this case, however, it is critical to take notes because emotional blindness is a very real thing. If you don't write it down as it occurs, you will not remember the vital details, and it won't be easy to bring them back.

The technique for finding shadows requires you to identify your shadows through the people who trigger you, specifically, your child. If you don't have a child, focus on a loved one, such as a spouse or a sibling. To help with this, I will use my 'needy' shadow to illustrate how I identified it as one of my shadows. I am doing this with the hope that you can learn from a real-life experience of mine. I will also use Scar from The Lion King to help explain some of the examples and emphasize the points.

As I mentioned earlier, I am triggered by whiny people who look for comfort and acknowledgment from others. I don't respect needy people, and I actively avoid them. This is why my daughter did not come to me and ask for help. She did not want me to lose respect for her.

Given this description of my shadow, it would be logical to conclude that I am repressing my need to be whiny, comforted, and acknowledged. Although this is true, shadow work is not that simple. It is a much deeper endeavor that requires a more comprehensive analysis. An analysis that deconstructs the trigger and my shadow into its piece parts so that I can figure out why needy people drive me crazy.

To deconstruct a trigger, you must analyze the triggering person (i.e., the person who triggers you) by looking at their behaviors, then their identity, and finally, their shadow. Deconstruction begins by analyzing the person's behaviors and speech to get insight into their personality. Please recall that personality traits are how you act out your identity, while shadow traits are included in the set of values, morals, and beliefs that constitute your identity. As such, personality traits are the external manifestation of your identity and are, therefore, the things you say and do in conformance with your identity. An analysis of the things someone says and does will tell you who they are. With that, we can get a good understanding of at least a piece of their identity. With the knowledge of how someone defines themselves, we can then deduce their shadows.

Our goal is to figure out our shadow from the trigger. The problem we have is that it is almost impossible to see the shadow when we are in the midst of the trigger's chaos. The first step to figuring out our shadow is to realize that a person has triggered us. Believe it or not, this is not always an easy thing to do. Then we must figure out what they said or did to ignite the trigger. The next step is to find the shadow that is manifested in the trigger, and the last step is to determine which pole of the shadow is true for us, i.e., north or south.

Now think of the thing your child does to trigger you. I suggest you name it and describe exactly what they do to set you off. Please write it down. It is important to also identify the specific behaviors your child does that provoke you. Sometimes it is not what they have done but what they have said. In a later chapter, I will describe a shadow of mine that was triggered by something the person did not do. Please remember, to fully understand what is going on when you are being triggered, you must accept the possibility that the thing you saw in your child is true for you as well.

The reason for looking closely at what your child has said and done is because those behaviors tell you about your child's identity. Knowing someone's identity tells us who they are. Knowing their identity gives us insight into their shadows because shadow traits and beliefs are significant components of a person's identity. Having a clear definition of someone's identity also tells us who they are not. This, too, contributes to their identity profile. Do not gloss over this step because you think you already know who your child is. As a parent, you probably do not have an objective assessment, so please try to be open and honest here.

Since a person's identity is composed of their morals, values, and beliefs, we can uncover their shadow by looking at those behaviors that are indicative of their morals, values, and beliefs. For instance, a person who will never tell a lie, is expressing a characteristic of their identity through one of their morals. It is also an indicator, but not necessarily proof, that they have a shadow around dishonesty. I would want to know if something significant happened to them during their childhood that is related to trust and honesty. It could be any number of things, such as a parent who always hid reality from them by sugar-coating everything. Maybe a significant and painful event in their life was caused by someone violating their trust, or maybe the person was punished severely for trivial white lies. The number of possible causes is quite large.

As we deconstruct the trigger, the operative question to be asked is, what type of person says things or behaves in a way that triggers me? If, for instance, we think back to Scar, the weak tyrant from The Lion King, we know that the things he said and did were evil, conniving, and reprehensible. We would need to know which of the evil and conniving behaviors triggered us. Knowing that he is reprehensible and evil is not sufficient. We need to know precisely what Scar did that set us off.

Details are essential. What did Scar say? What was not said? How did people around him respond to those behaviors? Maybe it was their lack of a response that will give us insight. As you ask these questions, you must tune into your feelings. Allow yourself to become vulnerable and feel your body. Become aware of and honor your emotional responses because your body will tell you when something is important and true.

You will rarely be able to decode the trigger the first time you experience it. You will have to be triggered multiple times to find your shadow. It is also very helpful to experience the same trigger through different people because it will eliminate personal bias against the individual and give you a basis for comparison. The objective is to deconstruct the trigger, see the pattern, feel the energy, and get a complete understanding of your shadow.

Please be patient with yourself and this process. Vulnerability and courage are also key.

Being triggered is not pleasant. Thinking back and re-living the triggering event can be just as upsetting as experiencing it the first time. Please do so with care and compassion. Meditate whenever you feel anxious.

If you are one of the few people who are adept at mindfulness and can observe the triggering as it is happening in the third person, that would be ideal. But most people cannot. In the next chapter, I will discuss mindfulness and its applicability to this process in more detail.

Please be sensitive to your emotional needs and only do what you can do. I know from personal experience you don't need to push yourself. Every time you are triggered, you will become more and more aware of what is happening, and you will begin to see the shadow dance more clearly as it plays out again and again in your life.

Once we know what type of person would exhibit those behaviors, our next step is to find the corresponding shadow. In some cases, we will clearly see the shadow in that person; in other cases, we won't be able to see the shadow because we don't know that person and their life story well enough. Not knowing the details of their life is not a big problem, however, because our primary objective is to find our shadow, not theirs.

The triggering person's role has been to be the model or template through which we can see ourselves and find our shadow. At this point, we can shift our analysis away from the triggering person and set our focus on ourselves. This is when we ask questions about ourselves and what is being triggered instead of asking about the triggering person's definition of self or their identity. To help with this process, I will often write a summary of how I define and experience that person as objectively as possible and then ask myself how and why that summary is true for me.

As I have mentioned before, many of us find it difficult to accept the idea that the triggering person is a reflection of ourselves. It challenges our self-image and identity in many ways. Keep in mind that we are only talking about a small facet of their identity that aligns with a piece of our own.

You should also know that there will be times when you will not be able to accept that their shadow is one of yours. Sometimes the shadow is simply too painful to accept; other times, it is because of the way you have framed and described the triggering. That is why the questions you ask and the details you uncover are important. Try to ask different questions by looking at that person and the triggering event from another point of view.

To help illustrate the questioning, let us presume Scar is our triggering person. In that case, we would ask questions such as, am I cowardly, and why? Am I cruel and a tyrant? Why am I that way? How do I exhibit those behaviors? Can I remember events in my life when I acted like a tyrant? What happened, and why? How did I end up in the circumstances that provoked that behavior in me? What happened in my past that caused me to believe those things or behave that way?

When you ask these questions, you will probably need to get into the details. For instance, the question 'Can I remember events in my life when I acted like a tyrant?' can be further broken down into questions about being oppressive, harsh, authoritarian, or dismissive.

Many of the questions thus far have been asked from the perspective of being the oppressor or tyrant. It is quite possible that you may not make any progress with this line of questioning because your shadow is actually manifested as its antithesis, i.e., not as a tyrant or oppressor. You will need to flip the questions around and ask the same questions from the perspective of being the victim of a coward or tyrant.

Please notice that these questions are designed to bring you back to those moments from your past when the shadow came to life in you. The answers to the questions are never as simple as 'I am that way' or 'I am bad, immoral, or evil.' The real answers are much deeper than that, and they explain the how and why of the shadow.

Also, remember to write everything down, even fleeting thoughts or images. Individual words, an object, or a person's face often pop into my head when I do this. They usually appear to be random or in total isolation, and then, after further analysis, they turn out to be the beginning of a thread that takes me deep into my subconscious.

If you find that you cannot go any deeper and uncover more meaningful answers, it is OK. Please know that your mind is protecting you from probing too far. Do not get upset or frustrated with yourself. It is a defense mechanism that keeps you from seeing things you are not yet ready to confront. Accept that as your reality and love yourself for knowing how to take care of yourself. Time is your friend. Eventually, you will be able to answer those questions. Merely asking the question and planting the seed in your brain is a significant step forward.

Earlier I offered my neediness shadow as a way to explain things with a real-life example. I will use it now to explain how I eventually figured out that neediness was triggering me.

Initially, I had no conception of shadows, neediness, or triggers. All I knew was that certain 'clingy' type people aggravated me to no end, and I avoided them whenever possible. I found over time that these 'Klingons' (I literally called them that) were aggravating me more and more, and I needed to do something about it. I became acutely aware that I had the same significant emotional response to many different people, but I did not know why or what they had in common. I began to realize that I was responding to behaviors such as attention-seeking, looking for acknowledgment, and whininess. Eventually, I was able to describe it as I do today. It took a lot of time and focus to reach the point where I recognized that their neediness was indeed true for me. It was my shadow too, and I could accurately articulate it. Formulating a description of the shadow in written form or as a picture and then saying the words out loud is a critical part of the process.

There was also a variety of triggering things that occurred in my life that contributed to figuring out my neediness shadow. For instance, I started to notice that I had strong emotional responses to TV commercials and songs. This was very odd because I did not have emotional responses to anything. One example was when I watched an advertisement for the movie 'The Greatest Game Ever Played'. The scene was of an accomplished, upper-crust man mentoring a teenage boy who was an outcast because he came from an underprivileged family.

At first, all I knew was that I had a strong emotional response to the TV commercial. That response occurred each time I saw the advertisement, and it surprised me each time it happened. That response told me there must be something important about this small movie snippet. Then I realized it was related to authentic, unconditional acknowledgment and the corresponding relationship between a father figure and a teenage boy. I eventually concluded that my emotional response was because I yearned for a father who would take an interest in me and offer a guiding hand. My father had died when I was a little boy. This yearning contributed to my realization that my shadow was not just about being acknowledged; it was much more profound than that. It was about being consequential to someone else.

I recognize that I just took a giant leap, jumping from mentoring to being consequential, with a father figure in between. The details of the steps I took and how I was able to make that jump from acknowledgment, mentoring, a father, and being consequential are beyond the scope of this book. You can read about it in 'The Inconsequential Child', a memoir I wrote that chronicles my journey to self-awareness and unconditional self-love. The important message I want to convey to you is that identifying and owning your shadow traits is not as simple as labeling the people who trigger you. Identifying the triggers is just the first step. A more in-depth analysis that deconstructs the trigger is required to understand your shadows fully.

Another critical thing to remember is that fear is not a shadow. Yes, fear can be overwhelming, and some people do indeed trigger anxiety and fear in us. But, fear is not the focus; there is always an underlying issue masked by the fear. Vulnerability and control are two places to look but certainly not the only places. Think of fear as a lighthouse beacon signaling you that there is something here. The shadow is in the nearby waters.

Mindfulness

*"Mindfulness ... helps us to be aware of and step
away from our automatic and habitual reactions to our
everyday experiences."*

Elizabeth Thornton

In an earlier chapter, I mentioned mindfulness as one technique I use when I am being triggered. It helps me cope with the trigger and focus on what is happening while I am under emotional stress. Mindfulness is a concentration technique of the mind where you become very aware of what is happening at each moment in time. According to Wikipedia ... Mindfulness is the psychological process of purposely bringing one's attention to experiences occurring in the present moment without judgment ...

Generally, mindfulness facilitates appreciation for life and your participation in it. For the purposes of this chapter, I will describe how I use mindfulness to facilitate awareness during times of chaos. My objective is to give you a basic understanding of mindfulness as I define it so that you will understand how it can be used to help you with your shadow work. If you are interested in pursuing this further, there are many books and videos available that describe different techniques for achieving mindfulness.

My use and description of mindfulness are designed to promote awareness and emotional stability. In this context, mindfulness is a technique I use that helps keep me from getting hijacked by the overwhelming emotional responses typically associated with a triggering event.

Usually, when I am triggered, I lose the ability to see, think, and respond rationally. My conscious mind gets hijacked by the events unfolding in front of me. Mindfulness allows me to combat that by actively focusing my mind on the present moment in a non-judgmental way. Through mindfulness, I can step outside the situation and look at the event from a third-person perspective. Once I can experience the event from the outside looking in, I am then able to see and evaluate all that is happening. I can then choose how I respond to the activities of the event as they occur.

The Wikipedia definition begs the question, what does 'bringing one's attention to the present' mean. It is the act of being consciously aware of the now. It is the conscious act of tuning into this and every moment, as the moments occur.

Typically, we live much of our lives in a 'default' mode, where we just react to things without thought. An extreme example of this is when we have driven ourselves to work and don't remember the details of the car ride. But this default behavior happens more often than we realize at the individual moment level. To illustrate this, I often ask people to think about the last time they purchased something at a store. The vast majority of the time, our attention is either elsewhere or nowhere during the transaction. Thinking back to that transaction, do you remember the cashier? Did you acknowledge the cashier during the transaction? Did you smile or look into their eyes and connect at a human level? Usually, we do not pay any heed beyond paying the bill as fast as possible. Those few minutes are lost forever. Once you become aware of mindfulness, you will see how much of your life is spent asleep as you function in the default mode.

The important things I want you to know about mindfulness are:

1. Mindfulness allows you to be conscious of the fact that you are here right now. For instance, you are reading these words, and you are now aware of the fact that you are reading these words at the same time.

In contrast, think of every word you have read thus far; you never once recognized that you were reading them. You only understood the messages that were being conveyed by those words as you read them. Mindfulness allows you to recognize both at the same time.

Mindfulness allows you to be in the now. As you read these words, notice the sounds and the activity around you. Notice how you are breathing. Feel the temperature of the air on your skin.

'Noticing' brings your mind into the moment. The human mind is capable of processing many things at about the same time. Mindfulness utilizes that capability to engage you in your life without also surrendering your full attention to only a singular experience. Mindfulness is being attentive to other things at the same time without negatively impacting the primary activity.

2. Mindfulness enriches your life. Frequently we respond to people without conscious thought: a nod, a grunt, a stare. Our response is an immediate default behavior that never reaches our conscious mind. Imagine consciously smiling at someone as you pass them in the street. Imagine that person's response. Some will smile back; others won't even notice. When you intentionally smile or acknowledge the smile from someone else, you have touched them, and they have touched you; both of you feel better as a result.

We have lost so many moments in our lives that we could have savored. When you are conscious of every moment, every moment is conscious of you, and you experience each moment fully.

3. Mindfulness enables choice.   When we are not mindful, most of our behaviors and decisions are made without complete thought. We simply do what we do out of habit and familiarity. We make thousands of little micro-decisions every day without realizing we do so. I call it default decision-making. However, when we live in the moment, every decision point is recognized as such, and we consciously choose. Like an orchestra conductor, we play our life's music by design rather than by chance.

4. Mindfulness is non-judgmental. All descriptions of mindfulness will include a caveat about experiencing each mindful moment without judgment. Authors will offer various reasons and explanations, but this is how I think about it. First, there is the event happening in your life this very moment, and then there is the conscious recognition of the moment as it is happening. In a sense, two things are happening simultaneously: the event and the consciousness of the event. For me, the consciousness of the event is the context that is happening around the event. When we evaluate, question, or judge the conscious event, we cause the two to merge into one moment, the mindful moment dissipates, and we are back to experiencing only the actual event. Being non-judgmental allows you to stay in the mindful state.

When I use mindfulness, I mentally step outside of myself and move into the third person viewpoint so that I can maintain awareness of the consciousness moment and can watch the event as it is happening. I never assign blame or judge any aspect of what is happening because I don't want to fall out of the mindful moment.

This ability to be in the moment and aware of the moment at the same time is a very powerful and beneficial thing. It allows you to combat the emotional hijacking that happens when you are triggered during shadow work. This is not like having a split personality where you can switch between the emotionally distraught person and the person who can analyze the situation without any emotional attachment; you are still you. Instead, mindfulness allows you to recognize that you are being triggered as the triggering is happening. It allows you to be attentive to the activity so that you can observe and interpret what is happening in real-time rather than be hyper-focused only on your emotional response to the trigger.

If you have never done this before, it will take time to develop this skill. In the beginning, just recognizing that you are being triggered as it is happening is a big first step.

Here are a few quotes about mindfulness that I hope will help you better understand it ...

"Life is a dance.
Mindfulness is witnessing that dance."

Amit Ray

"Training your mind to be in the present moment is the
#1 key to making healthier choices."

Susan Albers

"With mindfulness, you can establish yourself in the
present in order to touch the wonders of life that are
available in that moment."

Thich Nhat Hanh

"Every time we become aware of a thought, as opposed to being lost in a thought, we experience that opening of the mind."

Joseph Goldstein

"The ability to observe without evaluating is the highest form of intelligence."

Jiddu Krishnamurti

"The practice of mindfulness begins in the small, remote cave of your unconscious mind and blossoms with the sunlight of your conscious life, reaching far beyond the people and places you can see."

Earon Davis

"Look at other people and ask yourself if you are really seeing them or just your thoughts about them."

Jon Kabat-Zinn

"If we learn to open our hearts, anyone, including the people who drive us crazy, can be our teacher."

Pema Chodron

"The most precious gift we can offer others is our presence. When mindfulness embraces those we love, they will bloom like flowers."

Thich Nhat Hanh

Through mindfulness, you will become aware that you are being triggered and you will also see the subtle behaviors and energies that you are projecting. With this insight, triggers will have less and less impact over you because your attention will be focused on absorbing each moment as it unfolds before you rather than being hijacked by emotional turmoil. Being mindful, during moments of chaos, empowers you to effect meaningful change.

How does one become mindful? How do you interrupt yourself and become conscious of the moment? The following five-step process is what I have done to become more mindful during every-day life. You must first learn to become mindful during low stress situations before you can apply mindfulness to a triggering event. When you first attempt to do these steps, do not try to do all five steps at once. Master each step one by one. The process is:

1. Become adept at recognizing that you are in a relationship with someone. This sounds odd and obvious but it is not. For instance, every time you interact with a cashier, simply recognize that that is what you are doing. You don't have to do anything special. Just acknowledge the fact that you are in a relationship with another person at that very moment. When you recognize that you are in relationship with someone else you will probably make eye contact and smile.

2. Notice what is going on around you while you are in relationship with that other person. For instance, notice what the cashier is doing. Take note of what the cashier is wearing and what facial expression they have. Notice stuff such as smells or sounds. To do this you must step outside the interaction and look at what is happening between the two of you as the interaction is happening. You must also do this in a way where you are still fully engaged in relationship with that other person. Yes, this is not easy but it is possible to do. It takes practice and patience.

3. Identify how you feel, what you are thinking, and how you are responding. Are you angry because the cashier is making mistakes. Do you think the cashier is beautiful or unique in some way? Are you amazed at the bar code scanner technology? Or maybe you are worried that the people behind you are getting frustrated because you are taking too long looking for something in your wallet. Tune into your thoughts and how you are feeling. Those feelings and your response to the interaction are often automatic and without thought. Remember, this must be done without losing connection with that other person. It is possible to do this with calm patience and focus. You can do it.

4. Determine how you want to respond to the interaction. Maybe an acknowledgment of the person by smiling or complimenting them. Make this a conscious decision but do not yet act on it. Learn how to make the decision of how you want to respond consciously.

5. Make the decision in step 4 happen.

Mindfulness isn't difficult,
we just need to remember to do it.

Sharon Salzberg

Step 5: See Your Shadow

"The reason for evil in the world is that people are not able to tell their stories."

Carl Jung

Previously, we discussed how analyzing the triggers you see in other people can give you insight into your shadows. We walked through the use of projection as the first of two techniques to find your shadows. This chapter is a continuation of step 5, and it describes another method for identifying your triggers. Namely analyzing triggers from movies, art, music, symbols, or anything else that provokes a significant emotional response in you.

Please note that the things that trigger you do not have to be negative, dark, or evil. For instance, I remember a surprise going-away party given in my honor when I left my first full-time job. In hindsight, it was a wonderful gesture of appreciation and respect by many people. It was the first time in my life I was being acknowledged with genuine affection for merely being me. During the event, I was unable to speak and express my gratitude to everyone because I was overwhelmed with emotion. I was fully triggered and literally did not say a word because I could not maintain my composure. How I wish I had that moment to relive.

As a side note, I had not thought of that party in almost 40 years. It was not until I wrote this paragraph that I realized that it was a triggering event caused by one of my shadows. Unexpected insights like this will happen to you, too, now that you understand this phenomenon and you have a language to describe it.

The second technique for finding shadows is through movies, art, music, symbols, and even events like my party. The idea is to focus on any typical, everyday experience that triggered a significant emotional response in you. This technique follows a five-step process that was part of an exercise we did during the retreat I mentioned at the beginning of the book. Each of us was paired with another participant, and the activity required us to journal what our partner said at each step. After we completed the five steps, we gave our notes to our partner for them to read back to us out loud. That meant I had no choice but to express my thoughts and feelings openly, as they occurred. I am glad I did.

It is critical that you write down your thoughts and feelings with each step so that you don't forget anything. It is also essential that you verbalize them out loud. The objective is to bring each step to life as best you can by speaking the words and feeling the emotions. In the first half of this chapter, I will describe the process. In the second half, I will walk through these steps again, recounting what happened to me during the retreat when I realized that I had passed my shadow down to my daughter.

The five steps are:

1. Identify it:

   Identify the person, symbol, or thing that triggered you in the movie, art, music, song, or event. Describe it in detail, including all of the sounds, smells, actions, and emotions surrounding it. Give it a name. The objective is to bring it to the forefront of your consciousness without constraint or filter.

2. Point your finger:

   Express your reaction to it and allow yourself to feel it to its fullest extent. Speak its name loudly, and with the full emotion you felt at the time. Do not hold back. Describe why it is triggering you. For instance, what did the person do or not do that upset you? How does it make you feel? How is the trigger causing you to react? Call it bad names if need be. Yell at it if you are so compelled. Repeat the process of calling it by its name, as loudly as you want, and describe what happened and why it triggered you. Do this with the same emotional energy you felt as you were being triggered.

Notice the energy and the pattern it represents in you instead of just focusing on the specific actions and events. The objective is to feel your full emotional response to it. Feel its energy and try to understand its shape and substance.

3. When have you felt this before:

Identify when and where in the past you have felt this way or when you have been in the presence of this same feeling or energy. When have you reacted in the same way? Find a memory, a place, or a past circumstance where you could feel the energy of the previous step. See and describe the pattern at play. Details are very important to remember and describe. Also, try to find another example so that it can be seen and felt like a pattern rather than only seeing it as a singular event.

The notion of feeling the energy and pattern are essential concepts for this and subsequent steps. The idea is to remove the specific details from the emotion so you can experience its force and pattern rather than the event itself. That force, energy, and pattern are the template we are looking for so that we can use them in the following steps.

4. When have you done this to others:

Identify when you have done the same type of thing

to another person or when you have had the same impact on someone else. Be very specific. Describe the actual event, time, person, and place.

Think in terms of energy and patterns in addition to emotions and events. In some cases, your actions will have inadvertently or unintentionally resulted in you doing the same thing to others, while in other cases, you will have consciously been the perpetrator (i.e., the antithesis case). Ask questions such as, when did I do the same type of thing to someone else? When have I had the same impact on others? When has someone else felt the same feelings and energy that I felt because of something I did?

Keep in mind that doing nothing or ignoring something is also an act that may have the same result. Sometimes, doing nothing is more important than doing something.

5. How is this alive in you:

This is the step where you can see that the shadow is indeed yours, and you take ownership of it. The primary question you need to ask is about the existence of the shadow within you.

Here are some questions: When have I done it to myself? How does it manifest in my daily life? How does this serve me? How does it impact me? How is this same thing happening within me? Where does this pattern and energy dance in me? The objective is to understand how we manifest the shadow in our daily lives. Please remember that a shadow sometimes manifests in the form of its antithesis, but not always.

Give your shadow a name.

Before I walk you through these five steps again using an example from my life, I would like to mention the impact these steps will have on you. Specifically, you will see yourself and the world differently from now on. You will become more empathetic toward yourself and also with people who possess your shadow. Blame and shame will diminish. Forgiveness will be possible if it was not previously. These changes will occur because you are now more self-aware, but you need to commit yourself to being both vulnerable and honest as you do this work.

The remainder of this chapter is an actual example of me trying to figure out one of my shadows. It occurred during one of the workshops in the consciousness retreat I mentioned earlier. The workshop participants watched a movie the night before, and we did this exercise the next morning.

I offer this real-life example because I believe it will make the process more tangible for you and, therefore, I hope, more understandable. This example was provoked from a scene in the movie 'The Hitcher,' the original 1986 version. The film is an American thriller about a young man who picks up a homicidal maniac hitchhiker. The hitchhiker is on a murderous rampage as he stalks the protagonist and frames the teenager for all the murders he commits.

The first thing we had to do for this exercise was pick a scene that triggered us. I chose the scene near the movie's end, where the young man finally has the homicidal maniac in a vulnerable position. In this scene, the young man stands over the hitchhiker, pointing a shotgun at his temple. He cocks the gun, is ready to shoot, and then turns and walks away without taking the shot. This scene triggered me more than any of the other scenes in the movie.

I was very surprised that this scene triggered me more than the other more offensive and graphic scenes because I don't watch these kind of movies. I hate graphic violence and gore. I was also surprised to find out that I was the only one of the 30 participants to have picked this scene.

It is important for you to know how I chose this scene because it illustrates something I have learned over the years. Namely, the first thing that pops into your mind, before you have time to think about it, is often the most important thing to remember. This is one of the reasons why I have asked you to jot down everything that pops into your head, including the things that seem trivial, fleeting, and irrelevant.

When the exercise began, we were asked to pick a scene that upset us the most. This scene instantly popped into my head. Then, almost as fast as it appeared, it was washed away by many other more disturbing, appalling, and bloody scenes. Those other scenes seemed more appropriate to me for the exercise. But, I decided to stick with this seemingly less offensive scene because I was exhausted that morning, and I did not have the energy to deal with those more upsetting scenes. So, I picked what I thought was the least disturbing scene that would take the least amount of energy. Little did I know what awaited me.

Before you read any further, I want you to know that some of the language in this section may not be appropriate for some of you. I have altered the letters in the most offensive words.

1. Identify it:

   The scene was of a teenage boy, probably 17 or 18 years old, standing over a homicidal maniac, pointing a shotgun at his temple. The young man cocked the gun as if he was going to blow the murderer's brains out, but instead, he turned and walked away. I was outraged when the young man did not blow the homicidal maniac's brains out. I wanted him to take care of business and do what he had to do.

   Although I was outraged, I was not yet fully triggered.

The actual trigger occurred after the teenager took a half dozen steps away from the hitchhiker. That was when the homicidal maniac stood up. When he stood up, he vindicated my belief that the consequence of doing nothing would lead to something much more horrible.

2. Point your finger:

For this step, I concentrated on how angry I felt. I consciously allowed myself to feel the depth of my outrage and contempt. I sat there, feeling the anger grow within me. To my surprise, I started to yell at the kid in the movie. I yelled, "Be a man, you God d@mn f@#king wimp, be a man. Do what you have to do. Kill the f@#king b@$tard. Be a man! Be a man! What the he!! is the matter with you? Blow his f@#king brains out. Be a man; God d@mn you! Be a man!"

I was utterly incensed at his decision to walk away rather than do what needed to be done. I believed he had to kill the hitchhiker to protect himself and also because this guy was a psychopath who would kill more people if he was not stopped. My anger was intense, and I lost complete respect for the young man for not standing up and being a man.

3. When have you felt this before:

In the previous step, 100% of my energy was on the phrase, "Be a man." That phrase encompassed the energy flowing through me completely. It was all about standing tall and confronting something that was beyond my capacity to conquer but had to be defeated. As far as I was concerned, there were no alternatives. (Note: This explanation is what I meant when I said previously, *feel its energy, and try to understand its shape and substance, find its pattern*).

I was trying to remember a situation where I had to confront and overcome something daunting. Specifically, I was looking for a time in my past when I had to do something alone and with the full knowledge that failure was very real, probable, and catastrophic.

Because of the clarity of that phrase and the energy I was feeling, it was easy for me to see the pattern and identify when I felt that same way before. I did not need to think back into the recesses of my mind and find an event. Instead, a specific memory popped instantly into my head when I asked myself ... when had I felt this way before? The memory was from my teenage years when I was about 16. Close to the age of the young man in the movie. It was one of the many situations in my life when I had to stand up and confront danger, conflict, or some other hardship alone and with the full knowledge that failure would result in a devastating outcome.

This particular event took place in a parking lot in my neighborhood. My friends and I were playing street hockey when a kid my age from another neighborhood walked into the middle of our game and kept us from playing. We knew this kid. He had just won the Golden Gloves, a boxing title, and had been invited to try out for the US Olympic team. He taunted us and bullied the kids who were smaller than him. He was enjoying himself and was not going to leave. Someone had to confront him.

Even though I knew how to defend myself, I also knew he could easily beat me to a pulp. I walked up to him, dropped my hockey stick, and called him out.

I was terrified but did not show any fear. He turned and walked away. He said he did not want to risk getting injured because the Olympic tryouts were the following week.

The energy I felt with this memory was fear, elation, exhaustion, and anger. Anger because of the many times in my life, I had to confront difficult situations by myself, alone and without any support, comfort, or acknowledgment from a parent or loved one.

I need to mention that I did not understand the significance of the phrase 'be a man' at this point in the process, nor could I recognize the pattern. All I knew was that it led me to this specific memory, a memory where I stood tall, like a man.

4. When have you done this to others:

This was an unbelievably difficult and painful step for me. At first, nothing came to mind. I repeated the words, 'When have I done this to others? When have I had this same impact on others?' I said this to myself over and over again. My focus was on being a bully, and I could not think of any relevant time in my past because I have honestly never bullied anyone. I was going nowhere. Nothing was clicking. 'When have I pushed this energy on to others? When or where have I played out this pattern for others? When have I had the same impact on others?' Nothing clicked.

Then I asked myself, 'When has someone I know felt the same feelings and energy that I felt?'

Boom! My daughter Genevieve popped into my mind. When did Genevieve feel the same feelings and energy that I was feeling? I did not have a specific memory in mind but I knew it had something to do with Genevieve. At that point, I felt like I had been stabbed in the heart with a dagger of guilt. My beautiful daughter came to mind. This is the scene I described at the beginning of the book. I slumped into my chair, stunned, and I started to weep. I immediately began to formulate a new understanding of my relationship with my daughter, and it was very painful to construct and acknowledge. I sat with these thoughts, holding my heart with both hands. I just sat there, stunned, rocking back and forth. I began a Love and Life Meditation to call forth unconditional love as I wept.

Before I describe the new understanding that was taking shape and its relationship to my daughter, I need to describe the relevant part of the previous step that was the catalyst. Previously I wrote, *The energy I felt with this memory was fear, elation, exhaustion, and anger. Anger because of the many times in my life, I had to confront difficult situations by myself, alone, and without any support, comfort, or acknowledgment from a parent or loved one.* The operative phrase was ... *by myself, alone, and without any support, comfort or acknowledgment from a parent or loved one.* In other words, this was all about not being supported, comforted, or acknowledged by my parents. That is precisely what happened with my daughter. That is exactly what I did to her.

At that moment, when I made the connection to my daughter, I had no awareness of the process that was taking place beyond the obvious. I did not know what part of the previous step was the catalyst. It was only later, after writing all of this down, conducting an in-depth review and analysis of these steps, that I was able to figure out the operative phrase and its subsequent impact.

In terms of my daughter, my pain was sourced from

the fact that I was not with her the many times in her life when she needed me most. I was not there to comfort her in the presence of her pain and sorrow, and I, therefore, did not acknowledge her. I was crushed.

5. How is this alive in you:

    This was another very difficult step for me to figure out. The questions typically asked are about applying the action, event, or energy from the previous step to yourself. How does not being comforted, supported, or acknowledged by my parent serve me? How does it impact me? How is this same thing happening within me? When have I done it to myself?

    The problem I had was that I felt nothing. I asked myself if there is energy or a pattern existing in my current life around the lack of support, comfort, or acknowledgment? Again, I could not think of anything.

    I never felt alone, even when I was indeed alone. The concepts of support, comfort, and acknowledgment were completely and utterly foreign to me because I had no basis for understanding or internalizing them. This is because I manifested the antithesis of my needy shadow, which is not to be needy.

    For this step, I had to find times in my life when a normal person would need acknowledgment or yearn for recognition. I had to remember events when I needed comfort or support. I had to go back in time to that point in my past, where I could remember what it was like to need comfort and reassurance. But I could not. My neediness shadow developed when I was very young, and I did not have these memories, or they were so repressed I could not access them.

I could not progress this step beyond this point during the retreat. Weeks later, when I was home, I somehow figured out that I needed to feel the pain I saw in my daughter. I had to become my daughter in my mind's eye and in my heart. Only through her pain could I then find the pain from my past. I had to recall past events when I felt like her, invisible and unheard. I had to remember times when I yearned for the comfort of my mother's arms but to no avail. I needed my mother and father to acknowledge the pain and turmoil I was feeling in my life. This was exhausting and unbelievably painful work. Be patient and compassionate with yourself as you do this work. Time is your friend and the Love and Life meditation will also help you calm your soul.

Utilizing the 5-step process described above, I understood my needy shadow at a much more fundamental level. I uncovered the next layer of depth. I could see that I expressed neediness as its antithesis by never, ever wanting or expecting anything from anyone and by rejecting people who exhibited dependency or need of any kind. I also found out that I developed this shadow very early in my childhood, and it became a fundamental characteristic of how I defined myself.

I eventually realized the impact this shadow has had on my life. Specifically, it is abnormal to not need love, comfort, support, and acknowledgment. Human beings are pack animals, and our very survival depends on the depth of our relationships.

I grew up not needing people, at least to the same degree, as is normal for most people. I am, therefore, the atypical one. The needy ones are the normal people, and there is no shame in needing love, support, or acknowledgment. As time passed, I became more aware and comfortable with the idea that being needy is OK, and I began to redefine myself within this new context.

I learned one other very important thing; shadows can be multi-generational. It turns out that my mother was not only severely depressed, but she too carried the same shadow; as did my grandfather. I could only recognize that fact after having understood and reconciled my neediness, or lack thereof. A family pattern of dysfunctional behavior passed from my grandfather, through my mother and me, to my daughter. It is a painful reality that will not be passed on to the next generation because Genevieve is now aware of this shadow and its implications.

As you can see, these steps require courage, commitment, strength, honesty, vulnerability, compassion, empathy, and unconditional self-love. There will be times when you cannot make progress; don't give up. Emotional blindness is real. Remember the example of the person calling the kettle black. Please take note of what is triggering you, why it triggers you, and how you react to the trigger. But most of all, have faith in your ability to find yourself.

You also have to suspend blame and shame because they serve no useful purpose and hinder your ability to heal. When you do that, shame and blame will give way to acknowledgment and love.

If you decide to follow these steps for yourself, you have to be in a physically and emotionally safe and supportive place to work through this process. You may also want to partner with a therapist.

There is one last thing you need to do when doing this work. That is to speak in the first person. It is very common to describe your beliefs, desires, actions, and conclusions in the third person by using the words 'you' and 'them' rather than 'me' and 'I'. This is a subconscious act of avoidance. Speaking in the third person rather than the first person is one way we protect ourselves from the emotional pain of our shadow material. Speaking in the third person allows us to maintain some distance from the words and, therefore, avoid ownership.

Speaking in the third person is so common that I wonder if human beings have to go through a process of normalizing a painful reality before we can take ownership of it. By normalizing it, we must first make it true for the broader human community before we can conceive of it being true for us as a distinct individual.

Catch yourself when you speak in the third person. You must make a conscious effort to look for the words 'you', 'he', 'her', or 'they' and replace them with 'I' or 'me.' Always speak in the first person whenever describing things associated with you. This ensures you take ownership of it. Doing that changes the way you think and the depth of your understanding in profound ways. It is fundamental to this work.

Like emotional blindness, speaking in the third person is one of those things that is nearly impossible to recognize until you experience it. I remember asking someone who wrote a paragraph describing their trigger to replace their third person wording with 'I', 'me', and 'mine'. After sitting and rereading the paragraph a couple of times, she said to me, "I don't know how to change the paragraph." At first, I thought she was being stubborn. But that was not the case. She honestly could not figure out how to make the changes. I was astounded at the depth of her aversion toward accepting ownership of her reality. I said to her, "I want you to replace the word 'you' with 'me' or 'I', and when you used the phrase 'that little girl', write your name. She made the changes slowly as tears flowed down her cheeks, and then she said, "I see it now."

Finally, this is difficult, painful work that requires extraordinary courage and strength to pursue. Earlier I suggested that you envision a beautiful future for yourself. A future where you know who you are, a future where you forgive yourself, your parents, and your child. A future where you are full of unconditional love, are vulnerable and strong.

A future where the relationships you have with your family members are genuine, meaningful, safe, and loving. Please sit, hold your hands to your heart, breathe, close your eyes for a few moments, and envision that future for yourself.

Also, please don't hesitate at any time to stop and do the Love and Life Meditation. I use it all the time.

Blame, Shame, And Guilt

*"Whether you call someone a hero or a monster is all
relative to where the focus of your consciousness may be."*

Joseph Campbell

Many people believe emotions are either good or bad. Within
that frame of reference, they also believe negative emotions like
blame, shame, and guilt should be avoided whenever possible.
I do not support this belief system at all. I welcome all of our
emotions, both good and bad. Without the full spectrum of
emotions, we would have no means to compare and contrast
our life experiences and our lives would become unbalanced,
dull, and incomplete.

Emotions are neither good nor bad. They are like probes
that help us understand our feelings in relation to the people,
places, things, and events we interact with. They serve to
inform us about the world, similar to the way our five senses
inform us about the physical world we live in. Our five senses
communicate through touch, sight, sound, taste, and smell.
None of our senses is good or bad. They simply inform us that
something may smell bad, taste good, or feel hot. They are
windows into the physical world. Emotions are no different in
that they inform us of how we feel relative to the world around
us.

Blame, shame, and guilt are powerful emotions that can have
a disproportionate impact upon us if we are not mindful of them.
Blame is about being responsible for the pain that results from
something someone has done. It is the proverbial hot potato
that no one wants to hold. When we blame someone, we place
responsibility for the problem onto them. When we are being
blamed, we are charged with the problem and its resolution.

Blame in our culture has a powerful undertone of shame associated with it. The person who is to blame feels shame for having done the egregious act. It is as if blame is painted with shame, making the two feelings difficult to separate into distinctly different things.

Carl Jung once said, "Shame is a soul-eating emotion." I agree because it is a painful feeling of humiliation, self-hate, and dishonor. I also agree with Brené Brown's views on shame. She says shame is an "... intensely painful feeling or experience of believing that we are flawed and therefore unworthy of love and belonging – something we've experienced, done, or failed to do makes us unworthy of connection. I don't believe shame is helpful or productive. In fact, I think shame is much more likely to be the source of destructive, hurtful behavior than the solution or cure."

Shame is about being undeserving of love and respect and the legitimate subject of repudiation and rejection. I visualize shame as black tar or glue that covers us with a sticky layer of embarrassment and self-loathing. We are shunned by people who fear getting near us because they don't want our shameful residue to stick to them.

Shame is also frequently confused with guilt. Guilt is the feeling of regret for having done something wrong or for causing pain and suffering. For instance, I feel guilty about having ignored my daughter during her time of need, and I was ashamed of myself for being the type of person who would do such a thing.

Blame, shame, and guilt create a prison that is difficult to escape from because they are so tightly intertwined. Like all emotions, each should have a distinct purpose, but it is difficult to precisely determine what you feel and why when they are entangled. Instead, we feel a jumbled mess of self-hatred, regret, responsibility, alienation, humiliation, unworthiness, and hopelessness. If you feel one, you often feel all three.

Shame is the most dangerous of the three because self-hatred is at its core. Blame and guilt are the enablers or catalysts of shame. It is through blame and guilt that shame is delivered upon us so that we can inject ourselves with self-loathing. We are often in an internal battle between self-love and self-hate until shame arrives like a monster from the deep, spreading the destructive forces of doubt and unworthiness. Our hatred of that monster, and therefore the hatred for ourselves, overwhelms us, and we lose the fight. Self-loathing is the victor, and the spiral of self-destructive thoughts and behaviors takes over. All because of shame.

For these reasons, we must detangle blame, shame, and guilt so that we can see what each is telling us about our current circumstance. If we don't, we will be lost and helpless as we get locked into a chaotic cycle of unworthiness and despair, where each of them spawns the other two. In this tangled mess of confusion, blame feeds guilt and shame; shame feeds blame and guilt; guilt feeds blame and shame.

It is important to remember that these three emotions are fundamentally different, each with a specific purpose. Blame is about responsibility. Who should own the problem and its resolution? Shame is about humiliation, unworthiness, and self-hate. What makes you unworthy and dishonorable? What part of you do you loath, reject, and want to hide? Guilt is about feeling regret for something you have done. What do you wish you hadn't done, and why? To whom do you need to make amends?

Each of these emotions is different, with separate and distinct feelings. We must remember these distinctions when we are in their midst; otherwise, we'll get tangled within their grasp and not be able to free ourselves from their prison.

Like all emotions, blame, shame, and guilt help us understand how we interact with the world. They allow us to interpret right from wrong, and they can motivate us to be a better person, provided we do not allow the feelings of self-hate and unworthiness to be our primary focus. So, when you are feeling any of these emotions, become mindful and try to detangle them. Ask yourself how you are feeling and why. Determine what those feelings are trying to tell you. Break each of them down to their constituent parts and map them to the realities of the situation.

Here are some questions you can ask yourself:

1. What is the problem/issue?
2. What was your role?
3. Guilt: What part of the situation is your responsibility and why?
4. Guilt: What do you regret doing and why?
5. Guilt: With whom do you need to make amends?
6. Blame: Who should own the problem and why?
7. Blame: Who should own its resolution?
8. Shame: What aspect of this problem or event makes you feel dishonorable and unworthy and why?
9. Shame: What part of you do you dislike and reject? Why?
10. Shame: What are you trying to hide and why?

Like our five senses, emotions allow us to interpret our place in the world. They do this by informing us of our feelings as we interact with people, art, music, dance, nature, and everything else. Some refer to this as energy others refer to this as the language of the soul. In either case, emotions are neither good nor bad; they simply tell us how we feel as we interact with everything around us. They are probes that measure and interpret our inner world. For this reason, when I am feeling an emotion, I ask myself what is it trying to tell me. I want to figure out what I can learn about myself from this emotion.

I also think of emotions in pairs that exist within a spectrum where each emotion has an equal and opposite partner. Happy and sad are the easiest to imagine in this way. For example, imagine a strip of paper that is colored white on one end, and it gradually becomes pitch black at the other end. Now label one end happy and the other end sad. You just created a spectrum of emotions from happy to sad.

At any moment in time during the day, you can position your feelings somewhere on that strip of paper between the extremes of happiness and sadness. As the day progresses and you interact with the world, your position along the happy/sad spectrum changes.

Pride and shame are opposing emotions[4] that are paired in this way, too. This idea of pride and shame being paired is not a commonly held belief. The typical definition of pride incorporates the feelings of satisfaction and accomplishment derived from one's own achievement. Pride is also sometimes frowned upon in our culture because it can lead to conceit, arrogance, vanity, and narcissistic behavior. But at its core, if we remove its entanglement with conceit, arrogance, vanity, and narcissism, pride is simply about acknowledging oneself. Acknowledging yourself is a healthy form of self-love. In this way, pride is the equal and opposite emotion to shame, which is about self-hate. Pride is ultimately about self-love and appreciation, and shame is about self-loathing and disdain. They exist at either end of the same emotional spectrum.

Shame is an incredibly difficult emotion to deal with because it is about self-hate, humiliation, and dishonor, a place where no one ever wants to be. But, like all emotions, it is both essential and valuable because it helps us understand our relationship with ourselves and others in the world. When you pair shame with pride and place them on their emotion spectrum, it is clear that pride's self-love needs the counter-balance of self-hatred from shame. Self-love and self-hatred are equal but opposite

---

4   Pride, Shame, and Group Identification, Salice and Sanchez, 4/2016   https://www.frontiersin.org/articles/10.3389/fpsyg.2016.00557/full

emotions that are important ways for us to experience our place in the world around us. You can't have one without the other.

An unfortunate thing about blame, shame, and guilt is that people often use them for three detrimental purposes. One purpose is to use them as weapons to diminish others and establish that person's unworthiness. A second purpose is to manipulate someone to do something that benefits the manipulator. The third purpose is to avoid responsibility. In those contexts, blame, shame, and guilt can be very harmful.

Beware of others using blame, shame, and guilt as weapons to diminish you, and make sure you question the validity of their use against you for those purposes. For instance, is the egregious act you are being blamed for really that shameful, or have they blown it out of proportion? Also, beware that you do not do the same thing to yourself. It is very easy to fall into this trap, so please be careful and protect yourself from these needless, self-inflicted wounds. If you would like an example in today's society of how blame, shame, and guilt are used as weapons, you only need to think of the frequent use of 'privilege' and 'virtue shaming' to diminish and cancel people with different opinions.

When you blame others, you may be disempowering yourself. People often blame others so they can transfer responsibility for a problem to that other person and they can walk away. Notice that there are two parts of blame; fault and remedy. When you blame someone else, you are declaring them responsible for having caused the problem while at the same time expecting them to fix it for you. That means the remedy is solely in their hands. When that problem impacts you, then you become dependent upon them to find a solution. They now have power over you and your emotional state because they can choose if, when, and how to resolve the problem. Relinquishing ownership of the solution is both self-defeating and disempowering. If possible, never give someone else control over any remedy that impacts you. This is one of the ways to take responsibility for your life and empower yourself.

I choose to clearly distinguish between fault and remedy when I work with blame. I do not presume that the person who is responsible for causing the harm is the same person who must remedy or fix the situation. If I am harmed, I empower myself by taking ownership and responsibility for repairing the injury to me.

Finally, I'd like to discuss how to disempower shame. As you already know, self-loathing is at the core of shame, and its equal, but opposite emotion is self-love. Shame can therefore be disempowered through unconditional self-love. But how do we get to the point of loving ourselves unconditionally? One way is through forgiveness. Self-forgiveness of the things for which we feel shame. It is through each and every act of self-forgiveness that we will love ourselves that much more.

Forgiveness[5] occurs when we no longer need to avenge a wrong perpetrated against us. Forgiveness is not forgetting what happened. It is not excusing the act, condoning the behavior, reconciling with the perpetrator, denying accountability, diminishing the pain, or suppressing the anger. Forgiveness is, however, not needing to retaliate or punish the person who did the egregious act. To forgive, then, you must reach the point where you no longer require punishment and retaliation to feel at peace and content.

Forgiveness is only possible if it is unconditional. There is no such thing as true forgiveness if it has dependencies or contingencies attached to it. Either you forgive yourself, or you don't. And, you cannot forgive yourself if you are not completely honest and vulnerable with yourself.

---

5   American Psychological Association. Forgiveness: A Sampling of Research Results." 2006. pp. 5-8.

Fred, Luskin. Forgive for Good: A Proven Prescription for Health & Happiness. HarperOne. p. 7-8. ISBN 978-0062517210.

Honesty and vulnerability are the core requirements of self-forgiveness for the same reason they are a requirement of self-awareness. You must openly confront your past realities, which are housed in the recesses of your conscious and unconscious minds. Confronting your reality requires you to be truly honest with yourself which cannot be done unless you are also willing to be completely vulnerable. Only then can you begin to forgive yourself.

In an effort to make self-forgiveness more tangible, I offer the following personal example. Earlier I said that I am ashamed of myself for being the type of person who would ignore my daughter during her time of need. Shame tells me that I must, therefore, hate the part of me that has the capacity to ignore the real needs of others, especially my daughter. The act of neglecting my daughter harmed her, which in turn, had the effect of harming me. Recall the promise I made to my baby girl as she wiggled in her mother's womb. I said that I would protect her at all costs. Yet, I ignored her during her time of need. I failed her and myself at the same time.

To forgive myself, I had to find a way to eliminate the need to avenge the wrong I committed against my daughter. How did I do that? The first thing I did was to untangle the details and feelings of the event. The five-step process described in the previous chapter is how I detangled everything. Specifically, it was during step 4, 'When have you done this to others', that I was able to recall, in detail, what I had done to my daughter. I documented this in the scene on the first page of this book.

The second thing was to accept its truth, which included taking responsibility and ownership of it all. Then I needed to know how it came to be that I neglected my daughter. How did I develop the capacity to ignore someone in need? I already knew the answer to this question because I had already worked on my needy shadow. Specifically, I learned how to live a life devoid of nurturing and support, and that included avoiding needy people. I developed a blind eye toward them and their needs. I lived my life this way because I unconsciously knew I would never get my parents' comfort, acknowledgment, and support. I needed to do this to survive.

The next thing I had to do was accept that aspect of me that is incapable of giving nurturing, comfort, and support. Given that I had already done the work on this shadow, I know that this aspect of myself is the primary thing that allowed me to not only survive but prosper. This was true despite the fact that I was a neglected child. How can I not be proud of myself for developing this capability? Not needing nurturing, comfort, and support to the same degree as is typical of most people is a fundamental characteristic of me that I am proud of (and therefore love about myself) even though it is the cause of my daughter's pain. This fundamental characteristic of me is like fire; it can be used to cook or to burn. I must become mindful of its use.

Then I had to ask how revenge or punishment benefits my daughter or me. How does it serve either of us? It doesn't. I realized that punishing myself in any form won't provide any real, lasting value to my daughter or me. My daughter wants and needs the same thing I want and need for her; a father capable of providing love and nurturing. There is logically no need for retaliatory punishment.

The final step was to realize that I was both ignorant and blind when I perpetrated that act of neglect on my daughter. That does not make me worthy of punishment; it does, however, make me worthy of forgiveness.

Self-forgiveness is a self-affirming act of self-love. When you forgive yourself, you no longer have a reason to hate yourself, and you no longer feel the pain of alienation, unworthiness, regret, or humiliation. This is why self-forgiveness is a powerful and necessary part of both self-discovery and self-love. To quote a friend, "The ability to forgive yourself is infinitely empowering since it disempowers shame."[6]

And, all of this, love and forgiveness, are only possible if you believe you are worthy of them. This concept of worthiness is a fundamental requirement of self-love. Please do not doubt your worthiness, for you are a creation of God. If you still have any doubt about your worthiness, I want you to look deeply into your child's eyes; that glorious, beautiful human being. Look deep enough to see yourself. Know that your souls are intertwined. Now ask yourself, which of you is not worthy of love and forgiveness? If you don't have a child, know that your parent feels that very same way about you.

---

6 Peter was kind enough to lend this quote without full attribution in support of my desire to maintain my anonymity.

Sorting Things Out

"There is no coming to consciousness without pain."

Carl Jung

Before proceeding on to the sixth step of the process, 'Integrating Your Shadows', I need to address what happens when you find a shadow and accept it as yours. Until now, I have described it in very sterile and intellectual terms. In reality, it's not like that. Finding your shadow is an overwhelming, shocking, and deeply emotional experience. You may even become distraught at the pain and misfortune caused by not being aware all these years. One of the extraordinary realizations you will have is how pervasive the shadow has been in your life. You will be dismayed at your blindness and wonder how you could not have seen the shadow until now. Finding your shadow will lift a veil, and you will see things with surprising clarity.

When I first find a shadow, I am usually stunned and flooded with emotions, primarily sadness and remorse. I rarely feel anger or resentment because I don't hold animosity toward those who contributed to my shadow. This is because I understand how shadows come to be and why. Specifically, they are sourced from unconscious processes that are unknown to any of the participants. If, on the other hand, I determined that my shadow was sourced from conscious acts intended to harm me, I would indeed feel anger and resentment toward those people.

When the flood of emotion hits me, it comes as a jumbled mess of blame, shame, guilt, sadness, and remorse. I know from experience that I have to tease this mess apart; otherwise, I will be stuck in the inescapable whirlwind of all five of these emotions with no way out. It is imperative that I find clarity within these feelings so that I can hear what they are telling me. Each emotion is a probe with a different voice. The emotions of sadness and remorse will help me understand how this new shadow has impacted my life and the lives of my loved ones. That means I have to find a way to tease apart sadness and remorse from shame, blame, and guilt.

In response to my need to unravel the different emotions, I have developed the following process I call the 'Five Rs':

Realize: I am usually stunned at the outset. The words 'this is a shadow' literally pop into my head. However, if I have any doubts and am uncertain if the new shadow is true for me, I will drop it because that means I must not be ready to confront it. I will then acknowledge it as something to revisit and kiss it up to God for safe keeping. Please note that I did not say I reject shadows that are confusing, instead I give myself time. It is not uncommon for me to find shadows that I don't understand. Confusing shadows require more analysis, which ultimately means I will need to experience more triggering events to figure it out.

Remember: I will walk through the thoughts and activities that immediately preceded the moment of realization in an effort to remember and identify the behaviors or thoughts that illuminated the shadow. My instinctual reaction is to shut down my feelings and focus on something else. But I know I can't do that. I must become mindful, tune in and remember the details of everything from the past few moments. Remembering the thoughts and actions that illuminated this shadow is vitally important to understand what ignited the trigger.

Reveal: I will try to find distinctions between my feelings so that I can tease them apart. These feelings are usually overwhelming, messy, and inseparable beyond the pain. Blame, shame, or guilt; one, some, or all of them, visit me. My sadness and remorse are encased in the confusion of the three. The only way I know how to tease them apart is to honor my feelings and allow them to talk to me. So, I will sit in the Love and Life Meditation, holding my heart and weep as I feel their full force and depth. I try very hard to do this without any extraneous thoughts going through my head. I simply allow myself to feel and mourn my reality. This takes strength, vulnerability, and faith in my ability to withstand the pain unharmed.

Honoring and witnessing your feelings is the only way I know of to mourn your reality and gain clarity. If you doubt your ability to sit with your emotions, please listen to Dr. Joan Rosnberg's TED talk "Emotional Mastery: The Gifted Wisdom of Unpleasant Feelings" at https://youtu.be/EKy19WzkPxE. She describes the biological and emotional processes associated with unpleasant feelings and offers a 'simple formula' for moving through them. I wish I had seen her TED talk years ago. My personal experiences validate her message.

Reconcile: At some point I will slowly begin to have clarity. I will then try to tease out the sadness and remorse from the entangled mess of emotions by asking myself why I am sad and what do I regret. Nine times out of ten, my sorrow and remorse are about the loss of time. The lost opportunities to have been more connected with my child, my parent, and me. The lost joy and shared life experiences. My sadness is about the childhood I lived versus what could have been had my mother not been depressed and more aware.

This Reconciliation step is only possible because of the Remember step, where I consciously forced myself to recount the details. Without that memory and the specifics, there is no framework in which to tease out sadness and remorse, and I would remain stuck in the entangled web of blame, shame, and guilt.

Review: I review my blessings by acknowledging the fact that I found this shadow, a significant achievement. I spend the time to write it down before emotional blindness wipes it away. I am grateful that I have the means to heal it. I have the language to describe it and can share it with my loved ones. I know I am now a little more whole and aware. I am also thankful that I understand that there is no blame, shame, or guilt in any of this, so I don't have that additional burden. I know that the sadness I feel is temporary. It sits at a specific locations on the happy/sad spectrum, and I will eventually move past the mid-line toward happiness.

Sometimes, I will see the new shadow within my child. When that happens, my emotions intensify because it is no longer about me. It is about me being the monster that has inflicted this burden upon my child. I then get sucked into the pain and guilt of being an imperfect parent who has failed their child again. Although I intellectually know this is not true, I emotionally still get stuck in this hole. I have found that I cannot merely deny those feelings. I have to honor and acknowledge them, which means I have to repeat the Reveal and Reconcile steps with those feelings as well.

For me, this is ultimately a grieving process. I realize this may not make sense to some of you, but I don't know how else to describe it. I tend to have deep sorrow and remorse associated with my shadows. I allow myself the space to mourn the reality of the lost time and the lost opportunities. It is kind of like a death for me as I acknowledge and grieve the time and opportunity that will never be. At the same time however, it is a re-birth as I contemplate the new life before me. I know this sounds contradictory but it is my 'Amazing Grace'.

Amazing grace! How sweet the sound,

that saved a wretch like me.

I once was lost, but now I am found,

Was blind, but now I see.

Shadow work has been a blessing for me and I want it to be a blessing for you too. I hope the following experience of mine will give you an idea of the transformational potential this work can have. This example will illustrate how shadow work allowed me to escape the negative spiral I was in with my son. Through mindfulness and self-awareness I analyzed my trigger and converted it into a loving connection that healed our relationship.

There are two shadows associated with this example that I have not yet discussed. The first shadow deals with financial security; the second is a shadow that underlies my neediness shadow. I will not delve deeply into either of these other than to use them to provide context.

My son would often trigger me by saying he wanted me to take him to Disney World. We are Disney fans and were lucky enough to go to Disney many times during my kids' childhood. It is a place of fond memories with joy, love, and connectedness for us all. I, too, yearn to go to Disney World; the whole family does. But, we cannot afford to go given our current financial condition because of the cost of my son's college education. When he asks to go to Disney, I can see the glee in his face because he knows he pushed my button again. I instantly get furious because he is triggering my financial security shadow; a shadow I have not yet fully integrated. My anger turns to rejection, and I invalidate him and his request.

One day I was confronted with a painful reality about something else, and through it, I found the shadow that lies a layer or two below my needy shadow. As I was going through the Five R process, I made an association between this newly found shadow and my son's requests to go to Disney World. I realized that he, too, possessed this new shadow and manifested it through the Disney request. With that realization, I could clearly see that his requests to go to Disney were not wanton demands to selfishly spend my money and trigger my financial shadow. They were, instead, a cry for a deep connection and relationship with his mother, sister and me.

That realization was unbelievably painful for me. For years, I rejected his requests for an intimate relationship whenever he asked to go to Disney. My response to his yearning for connection was anger and rejection. Ohhhhh, the pain! Sadness, guilt, and shame overwhelmed me as I re-lived the times he would ask and I would reject him.

I now see those requests in a completely different light. When my son asks about Disney, my responses to him are draped in loving energy and acknowledgment rather than anger and rejection. I can do this because I now realize it is a request for connection. What was once a moment of conflict that was destroying our relationship is now a time to recount fond memories and connect. Had my rejection continued, my relationship with my son would continue to erode. I thank God that I found that shadow and made these connections. I have been blessed.

Step 6: Integration And Wholeness

*"Wholeness is not achieved by cutting off a portion of
one's being, but by integration of the contraries."*

Carl Jung

The previous few chapters described methods for identifying
your shadows including a five-step process to find them
within movies, art, music, symbols or everyday events. We
also discussed the projection phenomenon, which points us
to our shadows by recognizing our triggering responses to
other people. In this chapter, we will describe the process of
integrating your shadows into your consciousness as a means
for healing yourself and becoming whole.

The story of Dr. Jekyll and Mr. Hyde provides a metaphor
for shadow work by describing it as your very own personal
horror movie. The metaphor casts you as both the protagonist
and the monster. As the protagonist, you frantically try to
escape by opening each new door. At the same time, you are
also the monster that leaps through those doors terrifying the
protagonist. The moment of enlightenment occurs when your
eyes meet, and both of you are able to recognize yourself within
the other. This is what happened to me when I realized I was
repeating the same behavioral pattern as my mother. A reality
I did not want to see or accept.

Not being able to see ourselves as the monster is a blindness
that is both profound and necessary. It is necessary because we
need this blindness to protect us from believing we are horrible
monsters worthy of contempt and hate. It also protects us from
reliving the painful events of the past. The unfortunate side-
effect of this emotional blindness, however, is that we do not
learn from the monster and are incapable of developing the
knowledge required to live life differently. It is for this reason

that I said at the beginning of the book that *you are at fault, but there is nothing you could have done about it.* Your complete and utter ignorance of your disowned self has made it impossible for you to have parented your children any differently.

Logically it makes sense that we should not 'feel bad' about passing our shadows on to our children because we knew nothing about our shadows or their pervasive impact on our lives. Emotionally, however, it is not so easy. I know that I have felt and still do, at times, feel remorse and disappointment in myself for not having been a more enlightened parent. I have to remind myself that it was simply not possible. At that time in my life, I did not know of shadows, nor did I have the framework or self confidence to have developed the insights needed to learn about my disowned self. This is probably true for you as well. We need to accept our failings and forgive ourselves for being naively innocent.

I was hesitant to use the story of Dr. Jekyll and Mr. Hyde as a metaphor for shadow work because it is a harsh, exaggerated comparison. Mr. Hyde is indeed an evil, horrible monster, but our disowned selves are not so horrific; not at all. Nonetheless, I chose to use the metaphor because I needed a way to make the contrast between ourselves and our disowned self as extreme and tangible as possible. I wanted you to get a sense of its significance.

That moment of enlightenment when you realize you have a shadow that is indeed a fundamental part of you, is truly life-altering. It will shake you to your very core. Please recall the impact shadow work has had on me, my children, and our relationships. The two examples that I shared with you earlier, started off as extraordinarily painful events, and they ended as priceless gifts for my children and me.

I know this process of seeing your monster sounds so very frightening, but I want you to know that I look back on those moments with awe and the utmost appreciation. I consider those moments of enlightenment to be gifts given to me through the grace of God. As I describe this to you, I am frustrated by my inability to find the words to adequately capture how blessed I feel. Shadow work is painful, it is difficult, it takes time, and it is a lonely endeavor, but I would do it again, without hesitation. That is why I continue this work every moment of every day.

Through this work, you will find your disowned self, and you will wrestle with accepting it as part of you. This difficulty stems from the mental model or framework you have built to describe the world and your place within it. Your identity and self-image are a construct of this framework, and there is no place within it that allows you to incorporate all of the hidden and repressed traits and beliefs that you have disowned. There is simply no room within the identity you have constructed for yourself to acknowledge that the monster is you and that you are also the monster. Instead, you hold your disowned characteristics in contrast to your current definition of self; separate, distinct, and unintegrated. If, however, you wish to heal and become whole, you must make room in your framework to integrate your disowned traits so that your identity incorporates your monster.

Let me delve more deeply into this idea that there is no place within your self-image to put your disowned self. The concept of the disowned self can be thought of as the sum total of all of your shadows. Recall the characters Mufasa and Scar from The Lion King. They are complete shadows of each other and are, therefore, the other's disowned self. Together, they form one complete being.

In the context of the Lion King story, Mufasa's self-image and the way he defines himself has no room to hold Scar's biases, beliefs, and behaviors. And the same is true for Scar. He completely rejects everything to do with Mufasa's way of being. Neither can incorporate the other into their definition of self. Their self-identities are contradictory, and that plays out in the storyline as Scar plots and eventually succeeds in facilitating

Mufasa's death.

From the perspective of shadow, Mufasa and Scar are different sides of the same coin or poles of the same battery. They are, in essence, one individual, both the monster and the protagonist. Consider your reality; you, too, have two sides. The part of you everyone sees and the hidden disowned you that is unknown to everyone, including yourself.

Please recall the following quote from an earlier chapter...*If you stop for a moment and honestly think about yourself, you will recognize that this dichotomy is alive in you as well. You wear the mask of the good parent and accomplished citizen while simultaneously possessing traits and beliefs that you hide from others, including yourself. How can you live this secret life of contradiction? How can you be both beauty and beast? These are questions that probe deeply into the human psyche. This capacity to be both 'this and that' is an extraordinary characteristic of what it is to be a normal, healthy human being. Understanding the 'this, and that' reality and accepting its truth is one of the prerequisites needed to comprehend your unconscious mind's complexities...*

We now know that we are both beauty and beast because we hold our disowned self within our unconscious mind. When we are triggered, it comes out into our consciousness as rage, frustration, and pain. It manifests as an almost alien form that we cannot reconcile and integrate into our definition of self. But it is there, disconnected and connected to us at the same time. The question is, how do we integrate the two parts and become whole.

You are now at a critical point in your journey of self-discovery. Either you deny the existence of your disowned self, or you accept it as a fundamental part of you. If you accept its existence, you must find the means to integrate it lest you continue to live the life of Dr. Jekyll and Mr. Hyde.

The key to integration is to use our triggers to make our

disowned self known. This means making our unknown, repressed traits and beliefs known to our conscious mind. As discussed previously, you become aware of your shadows through your triggers. Your triggers act as the passageway or tunnel between your conscious and unconscious minds. Imagine that your triggers are firmly anchored at each end; one anchor in the conscious mind, the other in the unconscious mind. In this way, triggers link you to your disowned self.

Your triggers form the passageway or tunnel between your conscious and unconscious minds. As such, they are the conduit that transfers both enlightenment and pain into and out of your consciousness. Your instinct is to sever the link between your conscious and unconscious minds to stop the transmission of pain. Severing the link is something you have done many times throughout your life. But, cutting the link has not freed you from your reality, nor has it helped you heal or become whole. It has kept you in the dark, unaware and disconnected from the real you.

Instead of cutting the link, you should bring the anchored ends of your trigger together and merge them into a singular point that opens a portal between your conscious and unconscious minds. Memories and enlightenment will then flow freely, giving you access to all that is you. In this way, you and your disowned self become one.

How do you open the portal? You learn all there is to know about the shadow that forms the basis of the trigger. You confront it, and acknowledge it as an intrinsic part of you. Finally, you give it love and care, just like all the other parts of you.

Once you become aware of your shadows, you have but two choices; ignore them or integrate them. In reality, you only have one option because your mind will not allow you to ignore shadows or discard them from conscious thought; you can't un-know something. You will see shadows everywhere.

You will be reminded of your shadows as you watch people's interactions with each other. You will hear people blame others for their woes, and you will see their shadows as you are reminded of your own. You will listen to their judgments, jealousies, and desires, and you will see their shadows as you are again reminded of your own. You will see shadows in everything and everyone, including yourself. Your interactions, decisions, blame, judgments, jealousies, and desires will all reek of shadow material.

This newfound awareness of shadows appearing everywhere is like a curse of not being able to un-see. They are obvious and pervasive because your cloak has been lifted and you see what was once hidden. Over time, however, you will learn to see them as just one more manifestation of what it is to be a human being. And, you will treat them and the people affected by them with care, understanding, and compassion.

Since you have opened your Pandora's box of shadows, your only real option is to accept them as a fundamental, core characteristic of you and integrate them into your psyche. Why? Because the alternative is to live life as you have, unaware, easily triggered, and disconnected from yourself and your loved ones.

This chapter is about integrating your shadows into your psyche, which will require you to rewrite your self-image and redefine your identity. It is an assimilation process where your shadow beliefs and traits must be entwined into your soul as an intrinsic part of your conscious self. This can only happen if you are able to see your true self with all of its beauty and its flaws and then accept your true self with unconditional love. You will no longer be under the spell of shame when you can do that, and your repressed, disowned traits will not be hidden from you. They will lose their negative power as they become an integral part of the beautiful tapestry that is you.

Another analogy associated with shadows is that of an onion with its many layers. Once you uncover a shadow and integrate it, you will then find another layer of related shadow material underlying it. As an example, please recall the analysis of my needy shadow. Specifically, the fifth step, 'How is this alive in you.' During that step, I was trying to identify when I needed comfort from my mother. To do that, I had to be able to accept the idea that my mother did not give me comfort as a child. That is a painful reality that was not easy to accept for two reasons. First, my shadow so thoroughly repressed my neediness that I had no idea that I was ever in need of anything from anyone, let alone comfort, love, and acknowledgment from my mother. I simply did not know that I had unmet needs. Not needing love and nurturing from my mother is abnormal, and it defined me at a fundamental level.

The second and more important reason why it was painful for me to accept this reality is that it meant I had to be someone other than who I believed I was. It meant that I had to be an unlovable human being who was undeserving of love, comfort, and nurturing in my mother's eyes. This was a reality that was almost impossible to accept, lest it shatter my self-image and cover me in shame.

These two painful realities can be summed up as me being abnormal and unlovable because I do not want or need my mother's love, nurturing, and compassion. The wounds inflicted by that reality, whether true or not, are deep and the source of more profound shadows.

The point I am trying to make is not so much about my specific story. Instead, I'm trying to describe the phenomenon of the many layers of hidden truths. As you uncover more and more layers of your shadow, each brings with it another set of realities for you to confront and internalize. Each layer requires more and more courage, vulnerability, commitment, and faith in yourself. ,

The weight and burden of each layer are significant. Each new reality will cause you to change your worldview and redefine your identity. When you redefine yourself, you will need to envision yourself possessing more traits and characteristics than before. Shadow integration is an additive process where you become more whole. This will be a time of self-reflection and reconciliation as you accept this new reality and incorporate it into your definition of self. This process will take time, and you will need to be empathetic and compassionate with yourself and your loved ones.

Hopefully, through my example, you can see that redefining yourself requires you to incorporate new characteristics into your self-image. In my case, I did not redefine myself as abnormal because I don't need nurturing and acknowledgment. Instead, I redefined myself as normal because I need love, nurturing, and acknowledgment, just like everyone else.

I have to emphasize this concept and process because it is fundamental to the intent of integration. I had a choice to redefine myself as abnormal because I did not need love, comfort, and acknowledgment, or I could redefine myself as normal because I do need them. This is another example of the north or south poles of the same shadow. The abnormal definition meant I would not be willing to change who I am. The normal definition required me to change how I define myself and who I am as a person by redefining myself as being needy. Not needy like a 'Klingon' but needy like a normal, healthy human being. Understanding this thought process is imperative because it gets to the core of shadow integration. This change and redefinition of self is the only way to heal and become more whole.

You can do this, I am sure. But it will take time. Have trust in yourself.

As you know, not needing comfort or nurturing was a characteristic of my identity. It manifested in me as being self-reliant and independent. Through my external persona, I am known to people as being extremely competent, capable, and independent. No one, including myself, knew that this persona was sourced from my neediness. I am very lucky to have this shadow. It protected me from a life of conflict, turmoil, and unhappiness. Emotionally neglected children usually become severely maladjusted adults.

If being self-reliant, independent, and accomplished is such a good thing, why then do I consider it abnormal and a problem? Why would I want to change it? The reason is that this shadow impacted more than my ability to be self-reliant and competent. It also affected every facet of my life. Yes, it saved me, but it also limited me. It determined who I dated, the jobs I took, and the harm I did to my daughter. But more importantly, as I said at the beginning of the book ... *when you deny your reality, you deny yourself, and when you deny yourself, you are inconsequential.* Being inconsequential is the worst possible thing for me to bear. If that is true for you, I want you to know it is possible to overcome it. My first book documents the process I went through to recognize and then overcome my inconsequentialness. It also describes the beginning of my journey toward self-awareness, unconditional self-love, and wholeness.

When you integrate your shadow material, you change your identity, and your corresponding behaviors change as well. In my case, changing my definition of self has not only affected me internally, but it also affected my behaviors and my relationships. I began to ask for help, and I allowed people to comfort me. This strengthened and enhanced my relationships with them. Through mindfulness, I was able to recognize when people acknowledged me, and I thanked them for it; not an easy thing for me to do. In the process, I became much more connected, appreciative, and grateful for the people in my life, especially my loved ones.

Here is another personal example of how shadow work facilitates deeper healing by helping you uncover more layers of your reality. By the time I had undertaken the five-step process for identifying shadows, I had already spent many years working on my self-awareness and identity. I called it my journey, and I chronicled it in the memoir I mentioned earlier. As part of my journey, I thought that I had reconciled the fact that my mother was emotionally disconnected from me due to her depression. This was a painful reality that I had confronted and resolved, or so I thought. It was not until I went through the shadow integration process that I understood that the reconciliation I did with my mother was superficial.

As an adult, I knew that my mother had suffered from severe depression, but I still blamed her for my pain and isolation. My 'resolution' was to blame her for neglecting me, which reinforced my self-image as the victim. That is not a resolution. It merely shifts ownership of that reality from me to my mother. By blaming her, responsibility for resolution was now hers to deal with, not mine.

I do not know if the following is a quote from me or someone else, but it sums up my view on blame ... "Blame others when you don't want change, blame yourself when you want despair." I, in fact, had not resolved anything. I blamed her, disowned responsibility for my shadow traits, disempowered myself, and did not remedy anything.

It eventually became apparent to me that blaming my mother was nothing more than a way of sheltering myself from my reality and shifting the focus to her. Blame allowed me to avoid shame and guilt. In this way, I had no reason to find any resolution because my pain was transferred to my mother. Instead, I was left with resentment toward her. I had not integrated this shadow material even though I thought I had.

In an earlier chapter I said, ... *Our shadows are repressed and hidden deep within the jail of our unconscious mind. They are locked in by the bars of guilt, shame, and blame; kept repressed and concealed from everyone, including ourselves.* We will not be able to integrate our shadow and heal if our shadows remain under the jurisdiction of blame, shame, and guilt. That is why we must understand how they keep us stuck and unable to move toward wholeness. If we don't figure this out, we will never be able to assimilate them.

As discussed previously, using blame to avoid pain is disempowering. In so doing, we forfeit control of our destiny to someone else, and we become dependent upon them for our emotional state. This fact is not at all obvious, and it requires us to be diligent because of the ease with which we can fall into that behavioral pattern.

The healing process of integrating your shadows also requires understanding the difference between the behaviors resulting from the shadow and the shadow itself. Specifically, we are talking about the difference between the morals, values, and beliefs that make up your identity and the behaviors, actions, and words you speak in response to your identity. We discussed this earlier when we talked about the things you say, think, and do; and the fact that those things are consistent and compatible with your identity (unless you are suffering from mental illness). Knowing this difference will allow you to correctly differentiate between who you are and what you have done. Your behavior may have been wrong, but that does not mean that is who you are.

Integration requires you to incorporate your shadows and corresponding behaviors into your self-image. Earlier, when I redefined my identity so that being needy is normal, I also changed my behavior to ask for help and comfort. This example is relatively benign in that my shadow was not abhorrent, taboo, illegal, or immoral. If, on the other hand, my shadow and corresponding behaviors were taboo or illegal, this process would be more complex because I would have more parts and layers to uncover, reconcile, and assimilate.

Integrating your shadows also does not somehow mean your inappropriate behaviors are now acceptable or right. They are not. You did them, you own them, and they are a part of you. They are, however, understandable now that you can see them within the context of your shadows. Hopefully, seeing them from this new perspective will make them worthy of forgiveness; forgiveness of self as well as forgiveness of others. If not, you may want to kiss them up to God for a time when you are ready and able to make amends.

Please note that I did not say forgiveness from others. Instead, I am talking specifically about self-forgiveness. Requesting forgiveness from others is not required for shadow integration, nor is it recommended. This is because integration is about you, not them. It is an internal process that is not dependent upon anyone else.

Under no circumstances should someone else be in a position to affect your ability to integrate your shadows. You don't want to be unable to integrate your shadow until someone else forgives you. That is disempowering and unnecessary. You don't want to be dependent upon another person for your emotional well-being. Certainly, you can talk to others and explain the what, where, when, why, and how of your shadow, but asking for and expecting forgiveness is not required or recommended. It is also crucial for you to recognize that the person you ask forgiveness from may not be at that place in their lives when they are ready to forgive. It is unrealistic to have this expectation of them; they may never be in that place.

If, however, you are stuck and you believe you need forgiveness from someone else, please try to deconstruct how you are feeling and why. The chapter on blame, shame, and guilt may help. It is quite normal to regret the things you have done as a result of your shadows. And there may be a time when you need to reconcile with others. But, you must first integrate your shadow and become whole before any reconciliation can take place. Remember, forgiveness is about you, not them.

In my case, my needy shadow resulted in a variety of behaviors I now regret, such as my behavior to shun needy people and to treat them with disrespect. I feel shame, guilt, and remorse about acting that way, especially to my daughter. But my shame no longer includes self-hatred. My guilt and remorse are tempered by understanding my life circumstance, and I can forgive myself because I know why and how I developed that shadow.

Understanding how blame, shame, and guilt could bias my interpretation of my shadow allowed me to see things clearly and completely. I now realize that I no longer need to hold my mother in the light of blame. I can let go of that false reality and feel compassion and sadness for her burden of depression and the shadows she carried. To move forward, I needed to forgive her, and I also needed to forgive myself. Only then was I be able to integrate my 'mother' shadow material.

A significant shift took place in me when I realized I had repeated the same behavioral pattern as my mother. I now know, without a doubt, that I, too, was the oppressor. A truth I did not want to acknowledge or confront. An undeniable truth I could not immediately accept, a truth that pierced my heart with the pain of guilt. A truth I had to reconcile and forgive.

Until that point in my life, my self-image never included this type of behavior. My identity never allowed me to be the type of person who ignored someone in need or to treat them like they were inconsequential. Yet I did. I did it all the time and lived a life of delusion. My definition of self was obviously incomplete.

When I realized all of these things, a core part of my self-image was in shambles. The part of my identity that was fundamental to who I believed I was had to be examined so that I could redefine myself. I had to fit this new reality into my definition of self and then reconstruct who I am. My new identity had to include the fact that I have ignored others' needs and treated them as irrelevant.

The important thing for me to remember was that I now know I have the capacity to be that type of person, and I also have the choice to act in that way if I so decide. I may act that way again in the future, but it will be through conscious choice. This was a profound and empowering understanding.

As you redefine your identity, you too will see that you have the capacity to be the type of person described by your shadow as well as the type of person who is free from the shadow. Through mindfulness you will have the ability to choose to be one or the other; a profound and empowering capability.

The process of accepting and integrating your shadows requires you to define them without any filters. Clarity and wholeness are the operative words. You must see them in their purest form, as objectively as possible, without the tar of shame, the cloak of blame, or the weight of guilt. Integration includes acceptance without the self-loathing parts of shame. Stripped to their essence, your shadow traits are now easier to merge into your definition of self because the sticky residue of shame has been washed away with self-forgiveness and love.

To heal, one must integrate their shadows into their psyche, making those traits and beliefs an integral part of themselves. Integration involves assimilating the parts of your identity that have been repressed and disowned. You must love them unconditionally and merge them within as an intrinsic part of you. When you do that, it is impossible to feel shame about those traits, and there is no need to blame anyone or anything.

The process of loving your shadow parts will be gradual. It will not be an immediate, 'big bang' event. Over time, you will recognized that the intensity of your shame will diminish until it eventually disappears. This process will will open your heart to self-love and forgiveness.

Integrating our shadow traits requires us to understand them within the context of our self-image. When we redefine our identity, we must do it such that our formerly hidden, repressed traits and beliefs become consciously known and tangible. When they are named, real, and understood, they become like the other characteristics that make up our identity, and they become an intrinsic part of our psyche. These new traits are additions to the tapestry, which is you, not replacements. Our identity is, by definition, different than it was. It is bigger, more expansive, and more intricate.

Here are four steps that will help you integrate your shadow into your psyche.

1. Describe your current identity. This description should include your known shadows before you have integrated them within. Some people do this in written form; others are able to draw or paint a picture to represent their current identity.

2. Decompose your shadow and find its essence. Differentiate between the shadow trait and your responses to it. The things you did in reaction to the shadow are not the shadow. Find the antithesis or opposite side of the shadow so that you understand it fully and can appreciate how it lives in you too. Remember the analogy of the two poles of a magnet. This decomposition process may suggest you give your shadow a new name.

3. Describe your new identity with your shadow fully incorporated. Remember, these shadow traits are additions. You are not erasing anything. Identify how you will change the behaviors you described in the first step. Re-write or re-draw it with the shadow traits, beliefs, and behaviors fully integrated within the description or the drawing. If you want to change your shadow's name, do so.

4. Hold your shadow to your heart. Hold the paper with your new self-image between your heart and your hands. Close your eyes and say to yourself... "I am <insert shadow name>, and I love myself."

Finally, how do you know when you have integrated one of your shadows? You never will, and you already have.

I am sure some of you are saying to yourself... there he goes again with another one of his confusing statements. Let me explain. Shadow integration begins when you recognize that you have a deeply held wound that influences your definition of self. In other words, the moment you identify a shadow, you have started shadow integration because you can immediately see how your self-image is constructed around that shadow. Shadow integration is completed when that shadow no longer rules your thoughts and behaviors through unconscious means. When you reach this state, your responses to shadows are mindful and overt. You are fully aware and make conscious decisions rather than respond without awareness. Your shadow is no longer something that is distinctly different from you. You don't see it and respond to it as if it is somehow alien.

I would not be surprised if a few of 'you already have' started to integrate one of your shadows because you are now mindful of it, and it is a part of your conscious life. 'You never will' integrate it entirely, however, because there will always be another layer to uncover. I have found that I am perfectly fine in the vast majority of circumstances when my needy shadow would have previously been triggered. But every once in a while, something will happen, and I will get a little needy backlash of sorts. I have come to accept that as a healthy reminder of who I am.

Step 7: Share The Knowledge

"The most precious gift we can offer others is our presence."

Thich Nhat Hanh

In the previous chapter, we discussed integrating your shadows into your conscious awareness. The work of doing that can be difficult and painful but well worth the effort. The result of that work initiates healing as you unburden yourself from the weight and stigma of blame, shame, and guilt. Fear is also gone; clarity and understanding prevail. For the first time in your life, you unconditionally love this part of yourself. Time and acceptance are the elixirs you now need to heal both your heart and your soul.

Integrating a shadow is a monumental achievement; few have done so. Do not undervalue the accomplishment. Sit with yourself and contemplate the life you have lived thus far with that shadow ruling your thoughts and actions. You have completed your hero's journey and confronted a monster; marvel at your courage, strength, and humanity. You are an extraordinary human being. But your work is not finished. Now is the time to share this knowledge with others so they too can prosper, and you can strengthen your relationship together.

As we discussed earlier, some of you will have an overwhelming desire to tell your child that you completely understand them and love them just the way they are. You will want to show them how the two of you share the same shadow, and you will want to help them free themselves from their shadows. Your urge to do these things and more will be intense. But doing so won't be helpful. Trying to force your newfound knowledge onto your child may actually set the two of you back. Please don't do that, at least not yet.

When I realized that my children possessed some of my shadows, I was distraught. I desperately wanted to erase those shadows from them. I now know they must pursue their own journey of self-discovery because their shadows form their identity. If I could somehow magically erase them, who would my children be? They need to define their identity, accept and assimilate their shadows, and become the more expansive and intricate person they are meant to be. They must do this for themselves.

Instead of erasing their shadows, I can hold them for my children to see in a similar manner to the mirroring they did for me. I recognize that my children have given me an extraordinary gift when they held these shadows for me to see. In so doing, they have initiated me into self-awareness. The best gift I can give them is to acknowledge and accept those traits in me and mirror the integrated version of those traits for them to see. In this way, they, too, can become self-aware.

Through your example, your child will be able to see the shadows he has adopted, and then, he, too, can begin the healing process of acceptance, integration, and self-love. In fact, your child has probably already started to change in response to the changes he has seen in you.

Through the pursuit of your shadows, you have come to realize that some of your shadow material was sourced from your parents, and in turn, they were passed down to your child. You will develop a new understanding and appreciation for your parents, and hopefully, you can forgive them. In the end, through the pursuit of your shadows, your dysfunctional family patterns will be broken. Your children and their children will be freed from this legacy.

As we discussed earlier, you will have an overwhelming desire to fix your child and free him from his shadows. You will not be able to until you demonstrate that real, tangible change has occurred in you. They must see the change and believe you are being open, honest, and vulnerable with them, and that is only possible through action.

Keep in mind that your child learned about your shadows through the keen observation of how you have lived your life. You modeled those behaviors for them and reinforced their conclusions repeatedly throughout their life. Your only option now is to model new thoughts, beliefs, and traits. Your actions will speak much louder to your child than anything you can say. Your child has to see that your shadows no longer hold you hostage, and you are free from shame. The anger and resentment that is sourced from blame must dissipate before your child can believe that something in you is different.

Ultimately, you must 'walk the walk' before your child will acknowledge that something is anew. Do not forget that you are trying to undo decades of observation. The proof will be evident in how you confront and respond to those things that triggered you in the past. Your responses must be genuine because they are being observed both consciously and unconsciously. Your child will see both overt actions and very subtle changes, such as facial expressions and energy changes.

Your triggers will still trigger you, but not so much anymore. Over time, your emotional responses and energy will change for the better. Your triggers will have less and less power over you. You will have compassion for yourself and for the person triggering you. The energy of forgiveness and unconditional love will exude from you. Your child will feel it.

Don't Hide. Credibility, consistency, and authenticity are what are needed. Some of the people around you, including your child, will notice a change, but most will not have any idea that something is going on with you. You will notice that people will react differently to you in response to your change. Some of them will do things that sabotage your efforts. Many will be cautious around you; your child will be skeptical.

If you hide, or in some way, obfuscate the changes in you from others, your child will notice, and you will have lost credibility.

Be mindful and authentic in all interactions with everyone. When you are mindful, you are aware of the trigger, and you can make a conscious choice as to how you will respond. In some cases, you will choose to react as you did in the past; that is OK. In most cases, however, you will not. What is essential in both cases is that you are true to yourself in your response. Don't worry about making a mistake. Simply be the new you. You will falter, but those mistakes will be small when compared to the old you.

Don't hesitate to communicate what is going on inside of you. Allow your child to hear your discussions when you describe this process to your spouse or close friends. But don't let your child hear you say that your child possesses the same shadow. At least not yet.

Don't underestimate your child's ability to understand, and do not make any of it forbidden knowledge, except, of course, topics and details that are legitimately inappropriate or taboo. Use your judgment.

Think of yourself as a farmer planting seeds all around you. Every time you say something about your shadow to others, your child will listen and catalog what they hear. These seeds of knowledge will grow with proper care, and hopefully, your child will harvest the fruit.

There will come a time when it is right to discuss the shadow openly with your child. You will know when that time is. Speak primarily about it as your shadow and its impact on you throughout your life. It is OK to describe the parent/child relationship inherent in some shadows but do it in a non-threatening or judgmental way. And relate the situation to your parent and you instead of declaring it as your child's shadow. Let your child see the connections and commonality for themselves. Let them come to the realization that they share this shadow with you. When they are ready and feel safe, they will come to you and share their views and experiences of their shadows. Hopefully, they will also ask for help.

Prepare yourself for these discussions by observing how your child manifests their shadow. Make sure to see it as it is for them, not as it is for you or how you wish it to be. Determine how it lives in your child. Determine what side of the magnet they hold; have they adopted the antithesis, for instance? How do they respond to it? How do they repress it? What prohibits them from seeing it?

Here are more questions that may give you insights into how your child holds their shadow. These same questions will also provide you with insight into your shadows: What stories do they tell about themselves that you now know are insights into their shadows? What stories do they tell where they position themselves as the ultimate victim or hero? What people, places, or things do they ignore in the story? What do they rationalize as good or appropriate, which are not, when compared to family or social norms?

In summary, this is a passive process that allows your child to learn at his own pace. It is based on the belief that they will learn from you in the same way they learned of your shadows, i.e., through observation and modeling. They will also feel a greater connection to you simply because you have integrated your shadow and no longer express the corresponding negative energy. In some cases, you will even be able to eliminate a trigger completely, and if you are lucky, as I was with the Disney World trigger, the trigger will become a point of love and connection. Your child will feel acceptance and love from you as your responses to triggers evolve, and you feel love and acceptance for yourself.

Do not wait until you have fully integrated your shadow

to begin to share it with others. Your energy will be different, and you will model different behaviors as you start to figure things out. Try to be aware of this change in you and also try to observe how your child responds differently to you.

Finally, as I have said multiple times previously, I believe our children give us a priceless gift when they hold our shadows for us to see. Even though they may not be aware of their actions, it is a precious gift given with open honesty, innocence, and vulnerability.

I know by now, you have an appreciation for how difficult it is to see and accept your shadows. It is this difficulty that makes what our children have done for us so valuable. Treasure this gift because it is through them that we can see our shadows with such clarity. It is an extraordinary gift that our children give to us, and it is sourced straight from their heart.

Initially, I was in opposition to the idea that our children are doing us a favor by holding our shadows for us to see. I viewed it from the perspective of conflict and confrontation. I thought of it as my child forcing me to deal with my flaws when I did not want to see them. When I realized that holding my shadows for me to see in their full expression was, in fact, a burdensome undertaking, with a potentially hefty price, my point of view changed from confrontation and conflict to receptivity and gratitude. I began to see it as an unconscious act of love. My children were doing something for me that I could not do for myself. They gave me the opportunity to heal myself by allowing me to see and confront my unconscious self. Now it is time to return the favor.

If you recall, I have also said that our children are better off because they possess the shadows they have inherited from their parents. This is only true for those children whose parents can hold their shadows for their children to see in return. In other words, your child will be better off now that you know of your shadows and you have learned to heal. In this way, your child will know of his shadows and can begin to heal. Through your child's strength and love holding your shadows for you, you have undertaken your hero's journey. Your child will now be able to begin a hero's journey of his own as you hold his shadows for him. A slightly more straightforward task for your child because you will be there to guide him along the way.

Your Hero's Journey Of Self-discovery

"The cave you fear to enter holds the treasure you seek."

Joseph Campbell

Identifying and then integrating your shadows is difficult work that will take time and commitment. It requires courage, strength, vulnerability, honesty, and, most of all, compassion for yourself and your loved ones. But it is worth it. The benefits that result are invaluable, and they will change you in fundamental ways. When you can accept and love your repressed traits, it is easier to accept the shadows you see in others.

Your relationship with your child will become deeper and more meaningful as you do this work. Triggering events will lose their power and become much less frequent. Communication will be more open, honest, and direct because blame, shame, guilt, and fear are no longer ever-present. These changes will not be limited to your child; they will extend to your spouse, family members, and friends.

You will know and love all parts of your being because you no longer need to hide your shadows. You will become more whole, and your fear of being seen will disappear. As you evolve into a more grounded and complete person, your definition of self will become a more inclusive and accurate reflection of the person you really are. You will be more self-confident, humble, and balanced as a direct result of redefining your self-image and loving yourself unconditionally. You will no longer doubt your worthiness.

Your view of the world will no longer be biased by the filters that protected you from your shadows. You will see your loved ones and others as they really are because their shadows will be obvious to you. And, you will love them nonetheless. Clarity, compassion, and understanding will be ever-present as you interact with others and you see their vulnerability.

Your creativity will flourish, and you will feel free to express and create because the shackles of shame and fear will not hinder you. You will be on a life-long journey of self-discovery: a journey that will bring you joy, purpose, and unconditional love.

You will be able to hold everyone in your life with compassionate arms, and you will see them. Truly see them as they are. They will be witnessed and understood by you as you hold them in unconditional love.

The future you imagined at the beginning of this book is there waiting for you. It is a beautiful future where you come to know who you are and why. A future where you forgive yourself, your parents, and your child. A future where you are full of unconditional love, are vulnerable and strong. A future where the relationships you have with your family members are real and meaningful. This future is yours.

I hope this book has helped you understand the nature of the relationship you have with your child and also with yourself. A complicated relationship that I described as a shadow dance. An intricate dance of grace and love that will hopefully foster healthier, more meaningful relationships with you and your loved ones. May God bless you and yours.

With love,

me

Printed in Great Britain
by Amazon

37220278R00089